The Football Maths Book

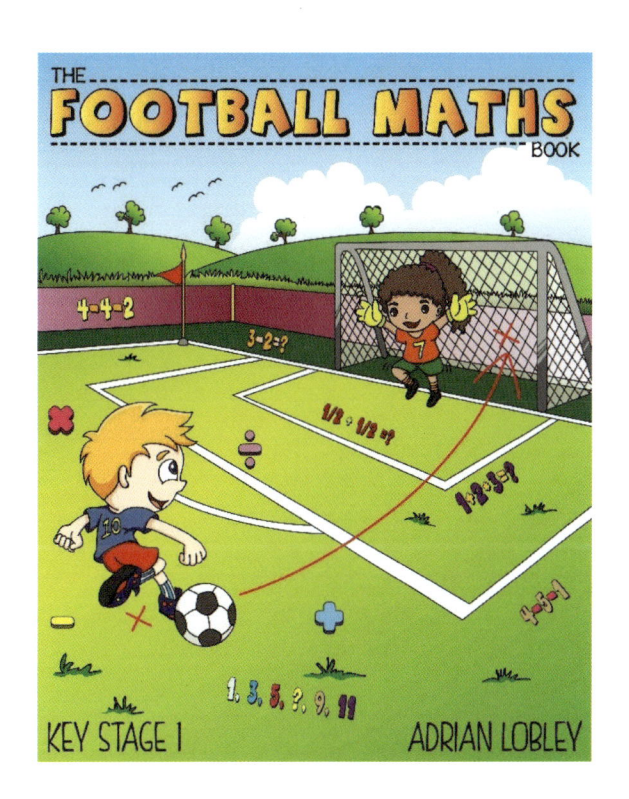

Adrian Lobley

To Sebastian

With thanks to:
Sebastian Wraith-Lobley
Beverley Harris
Sarah Wraith
Nick Callaghan
Malcolm Lobley
Joshua Clements
Christopher Chamberlain
Hayden Cowan
Finlay Cronshaw
Miss Pugh

Front/back cover illustrations by:
Alyssa Josue

Copyright © 2015 Adrian Lobley
All rights reserved.
ISBN-13: 978-1519133137
ISBN-10: 1519133138

Fill in the missing numbers on the shirts.

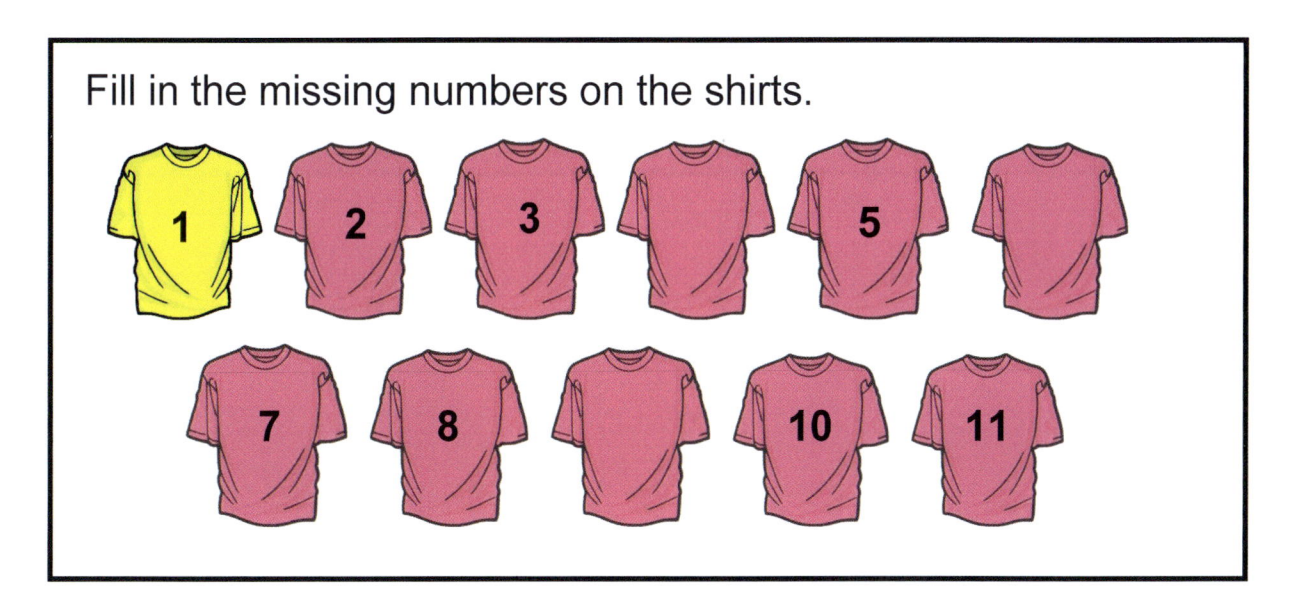

1 2 3 ☐ 5 ☐
7 8 ☐ 10 11

The goalkeeper always wears a different coloured shirt

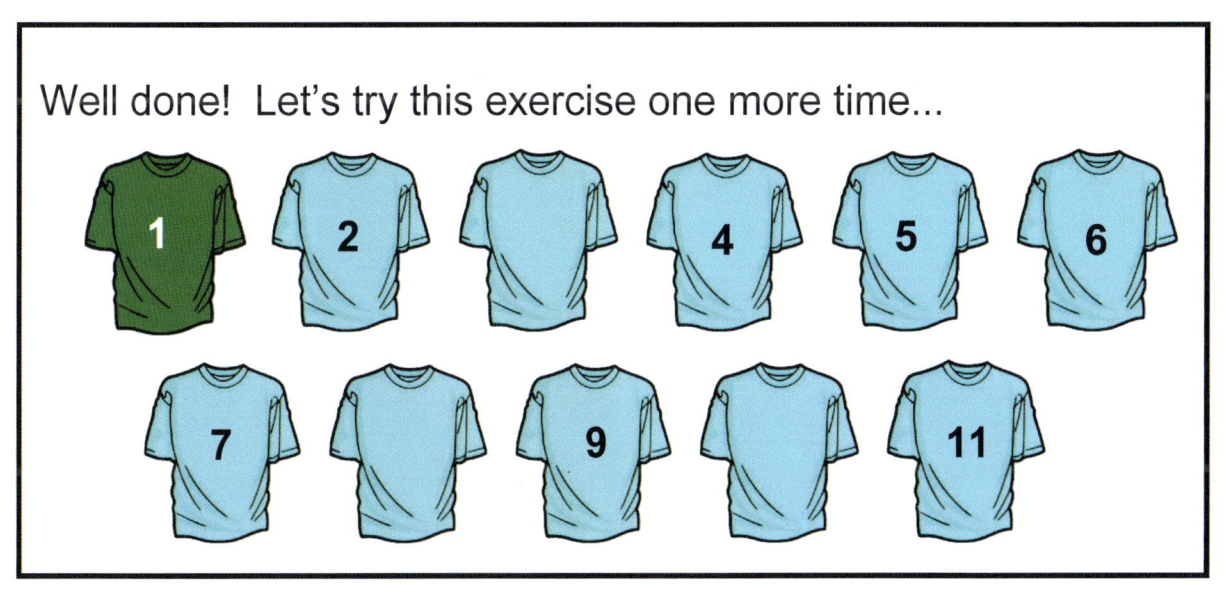

Well done! Let's try this exercise one more time...

1 2 ☐ 4 5 6
7 ☐ 9 ☐ 11

Write your match score for this page by entering the number of shirts you got right and wrong here: ☐ — ☐

1

Below is an 11-a-side team. The players who wear these shirts tend to stay in that position on the football field. Draw a line from 1 to 2. Then link it to 3. Then to 4 and so on…up to 11.

Attackers: 10, 9

Midfielders: 11, 4, 8, 7

Defenders: 3, 5, 6, 2

Goalkeeper: 1

Write your match score for this page by entering the number of links you got right and wrong here: ☐ — ☐

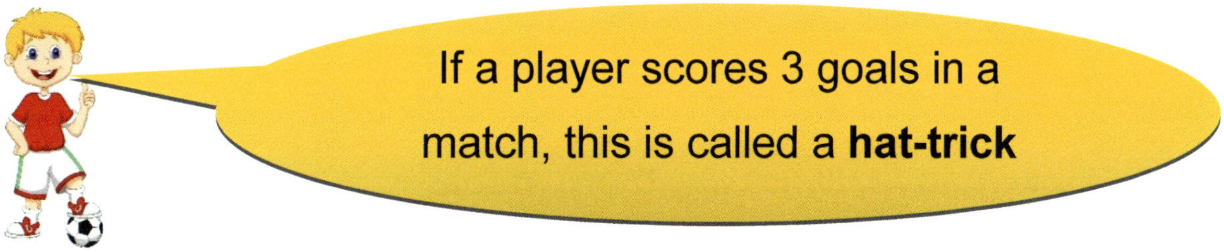

If a player scores 3 goals in a match, this is called a **hat-trick**

If a player scores a **hat-trick** in his first match and then 1 goal in his next match, how many goals has the player scored in total?

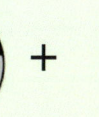

3 + 1 = ☐

If a player scores 2 hat-tricks, how many goals has he scored?

3 + 3 = ☐

Write your match score for this page by entering the number of questions you got right and wrong here: ☐ — ☐

In a 5-a-side match, there are 2 teams with 5 players in each team. How many players are there in total?

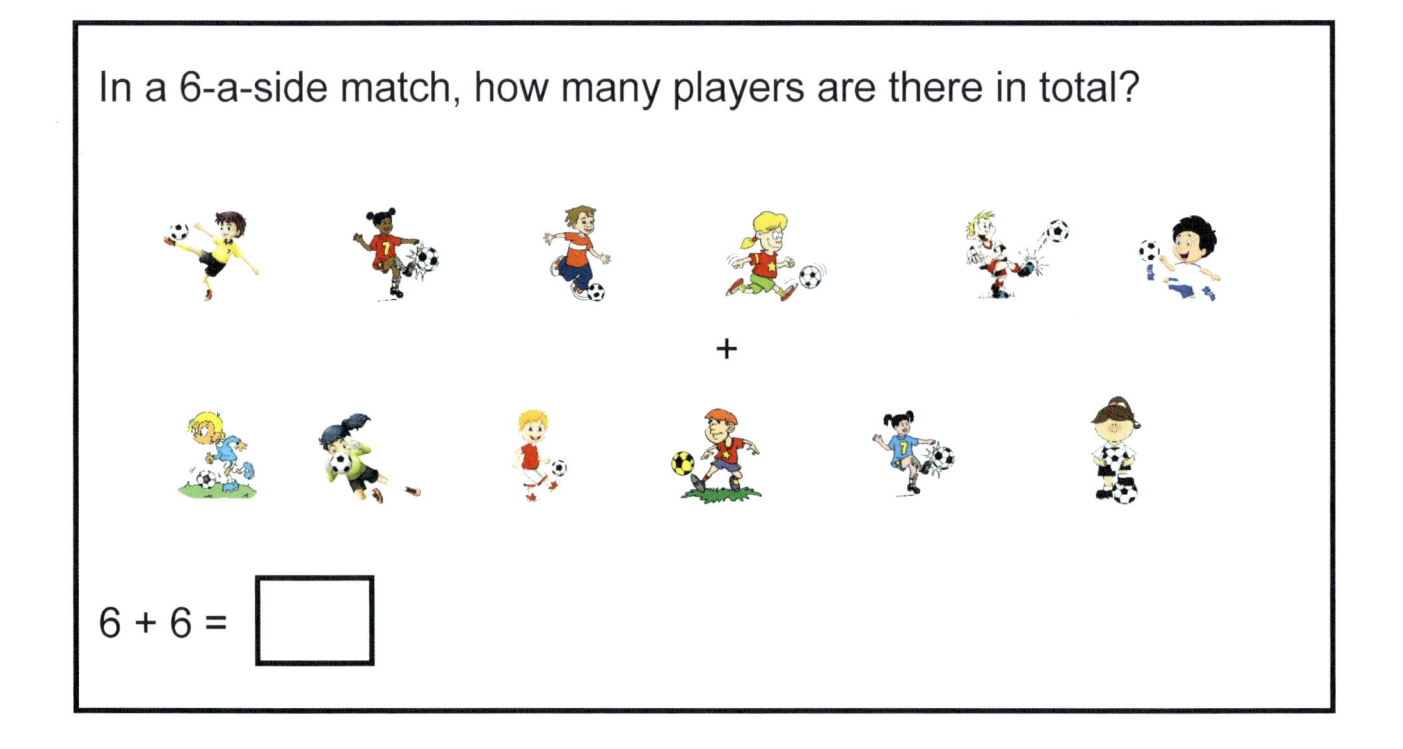

5 + 5 = ☐

In a 6-a-side match, how many players are there in total?

6 + 6 = ☐

Enter your match score for this page: ☐ — ☐

Use the number line below to help you with this question

If a team wins 3-1 then they have won by 2 goals because 3 - 1 = 2

How many goals did the following teams win by?

United   won   4 – 1   ☐
City   won   4 – 2   ☐
Town   won   2 – 0   ☐

```
0   1   2   3   4   5   6
|   |   |   |   |   |   |
```

How many goals did the following teams win by?

Albion   won   2 – 1   ☐
Rovers   won   5 – 3   ☐
Argyle   won   6 – 2   ☐

Enter your score for the 6 questions above: ☐ — ☐

5

If a cup match finishes as a draw then the 2 teams often contest a penalty shoot-out, to find out who the winner will be.

A cup match is a one-off match between 2 teams

A green circle = penalty scored.
A red circle = penalty missed.

Below City have 3 green circles and 2 red circles so they scored 3 penalties. Enter in the box the number of penalties United scored.

City 🟢 🟢 🔴 🟢 🔴 = 3

United 🟢 🔴 🟢 🟢 🟢 = ☐

Which team won? ☐

Both boxes correct? Enter your score: ☐ — ☐

What is the penalty shoot-out score here?

Town 🔴 🟢 🔴 🟢 🟢 = ☐

Argyle 🟢 🟢 🔴 🔴 🔴 = ☐

Which team won? ☐

What is the penalty shoot-out score here?

County 🟢 🔴 🟢 🟢 🟢 = ☐

Albion 🔴 🟢 🔴 🔴 🟢 = ☐

Which team won? ☐

All 6 boxes correct? Enter your score: ☐ — ☐

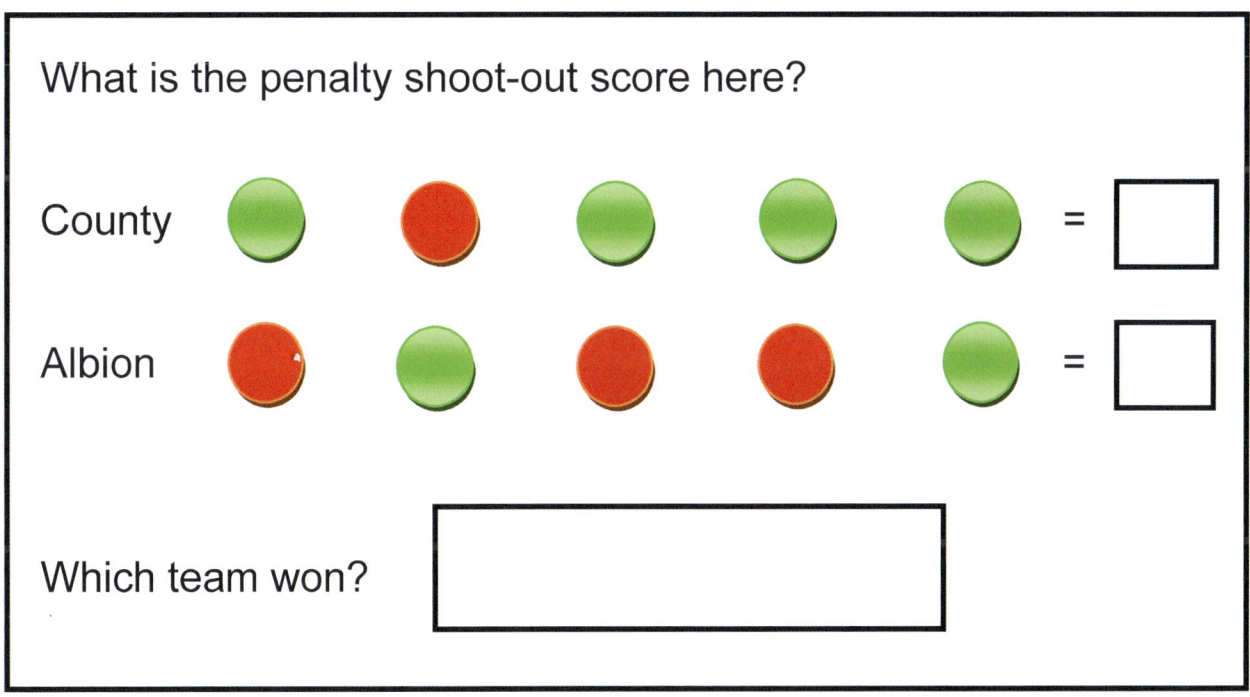

One of United's players scored a hat-trick (i.e. 3 goals) in one of these 3 matches. Which match did he score the hat-trick in? Tick the only box it can be.

United 2 – 0   City   ☐
United 1 – 1   Town   ☐
United 3 – 2   Wanderers   ☐

One of United's players scored a hat-trick in one of these matches. Which match did he score the hat-trick in?

United 1 – 0   Argyle   ☐
United 4 – 2   Albion   ☐
United 2 – 2   Palace   ☐

Enter your score for this page: ☐ – ☐

Cross out half (½) of the footballs in each set below. Enter the number remaining.

How many players are there in the picture below? ☐

Cross out half (½) of the players.

How many players remain? ☐

Enter your score for this page: ☐ — ☐

Keep doubling the score below

1 – 0

☐ – ☐

☐ – ☐

☐ – ☐

Double the scores below, in the boxes opposite.

2 – 0 ⟶ ☐ – ☐

3 – 0 ⟶ ☐ – ☐

1 – 1 ⟶ ☐ – ☐

1 – 2 ⟶ ☐ – ☐

2 – 3 ⟶ ☐ – ☐

Enter your score for this page: ☐ – ☐

> Use the number line below, to help you with this question

If a team wins a league match they get 3 points. If they get a draw, they get 1 point. They get 0 points if they lose. Fill in the number of points under each result. Then add them up.

City   Draw + Draw   =   Total ☐

United   Win + Win   = ☐

Wanderers   Win + Loss   = ☐

Number line

0   1   2   3   4   5   6   7   8   9   10

Enter your score for this page: ☐ — ☐

If a team wins a league match they get 3 points. If they get a draw, they get 1 point. They get 0 points if they lose. Fill in the number of points under each result. Then add them up.

City Draw + Draw + Draw = Total
☐ ☐ ☐ = ☐

United Win + Draw + Loss
☐ ☐ ☐ = ☐

Wanderers Win + Draw + Win
☐ ☐ ☐ = ☐

Number line
0 1 2 3 4 5 6 7 8 9 10

Enter your score for this page: ☐ — ☐

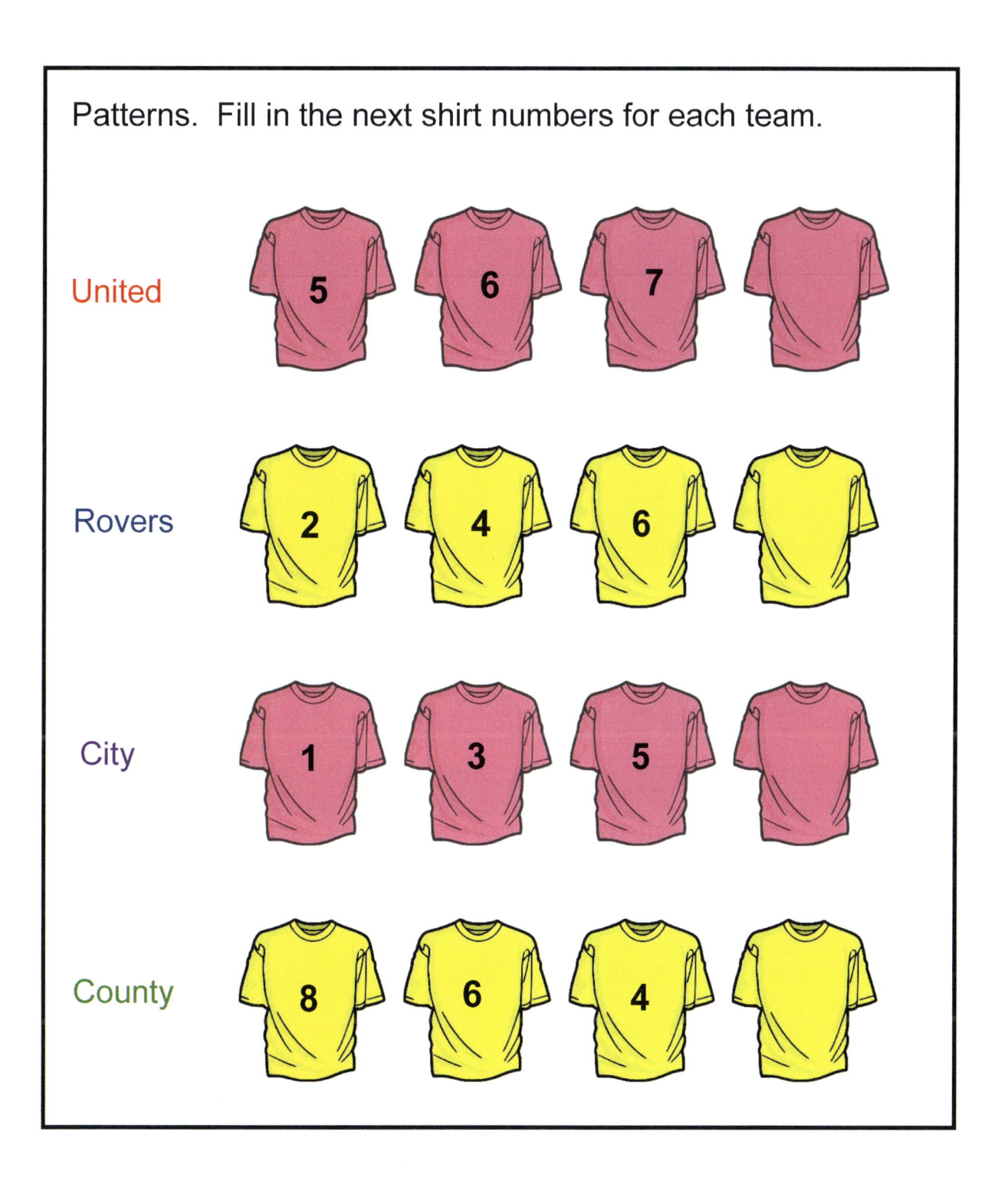

Patterns. Fill in the next shirt numbers for each team.

United: 5, 6, 7, ___

Rovers: 2, 4, 6, ___

City: 1, 3, 5, ___

County: 8, 6, 4, ___

Enter your score for this page: ☐ — ☐

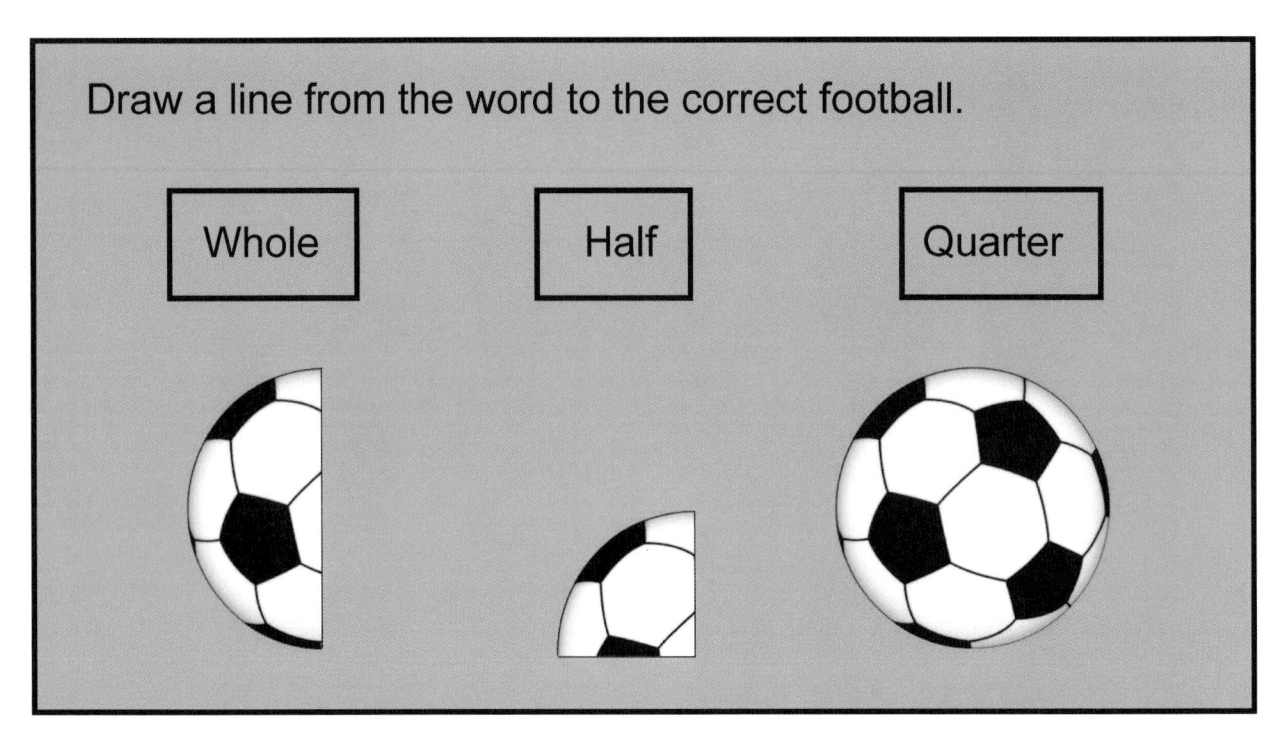

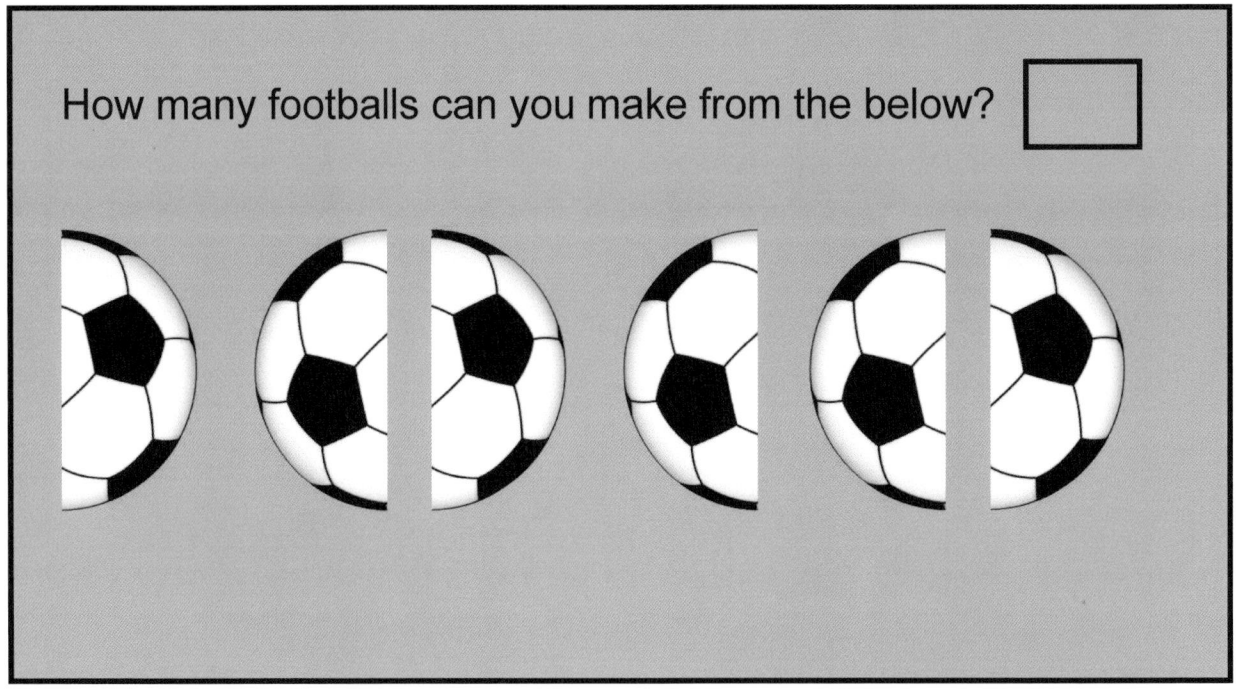

Draw a line from the word to the correct football.

| Whole | Half | Quarter |

How many footballs can you make from the below?

Enter your score for this page:

14

Write **odd** or **even** in the box next to the shirt number.

- 1 ☐
- 4 ☐
- 8 ☐
- 5 ☐
- 7 ☐
- 9 ☐

Enter your score for this page: ☐ — ☐

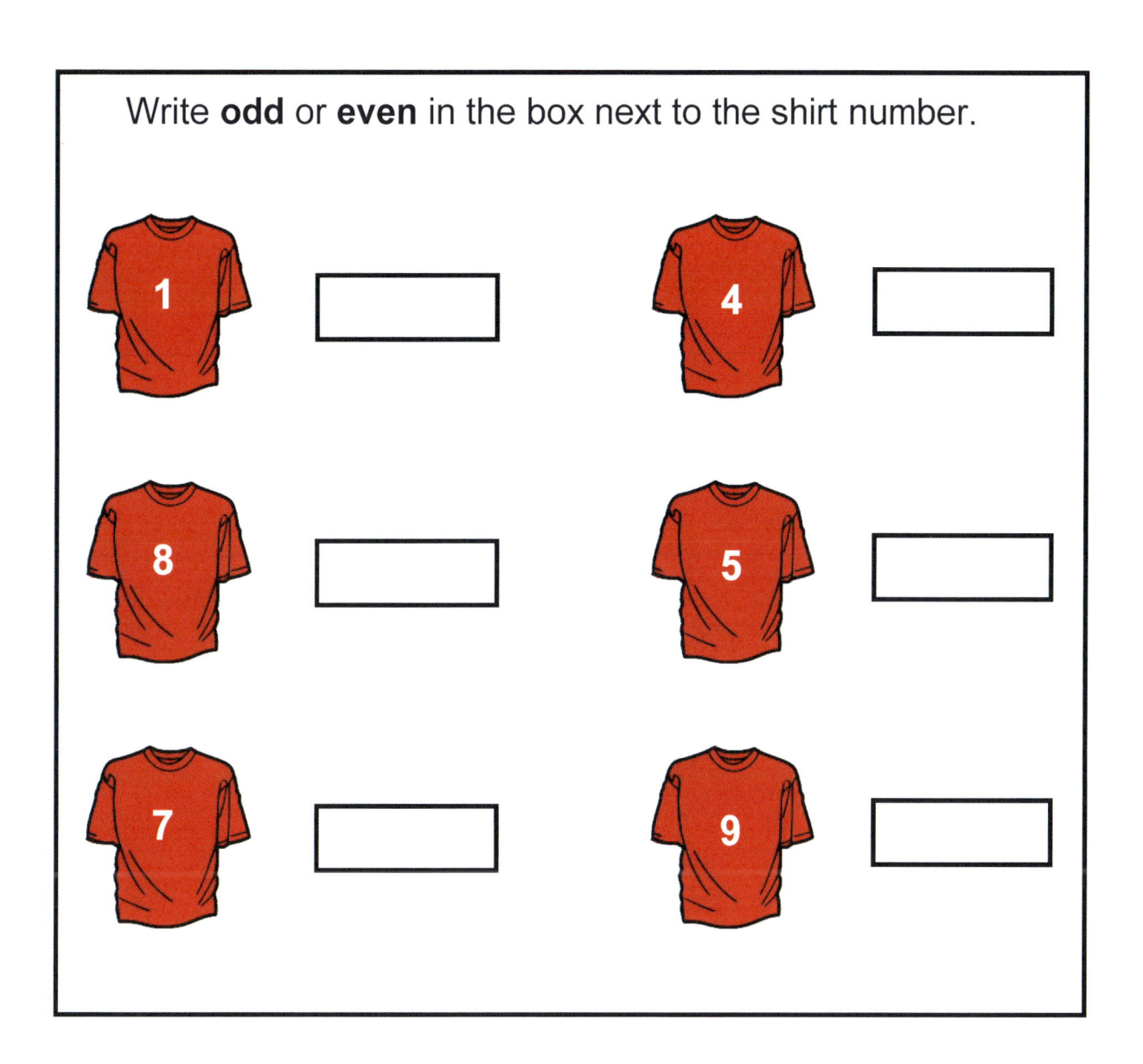

Keep halving the score below

8 – 0

☐ – ☐

☐ – ☐

☐ – ☐

Half of zero is zero

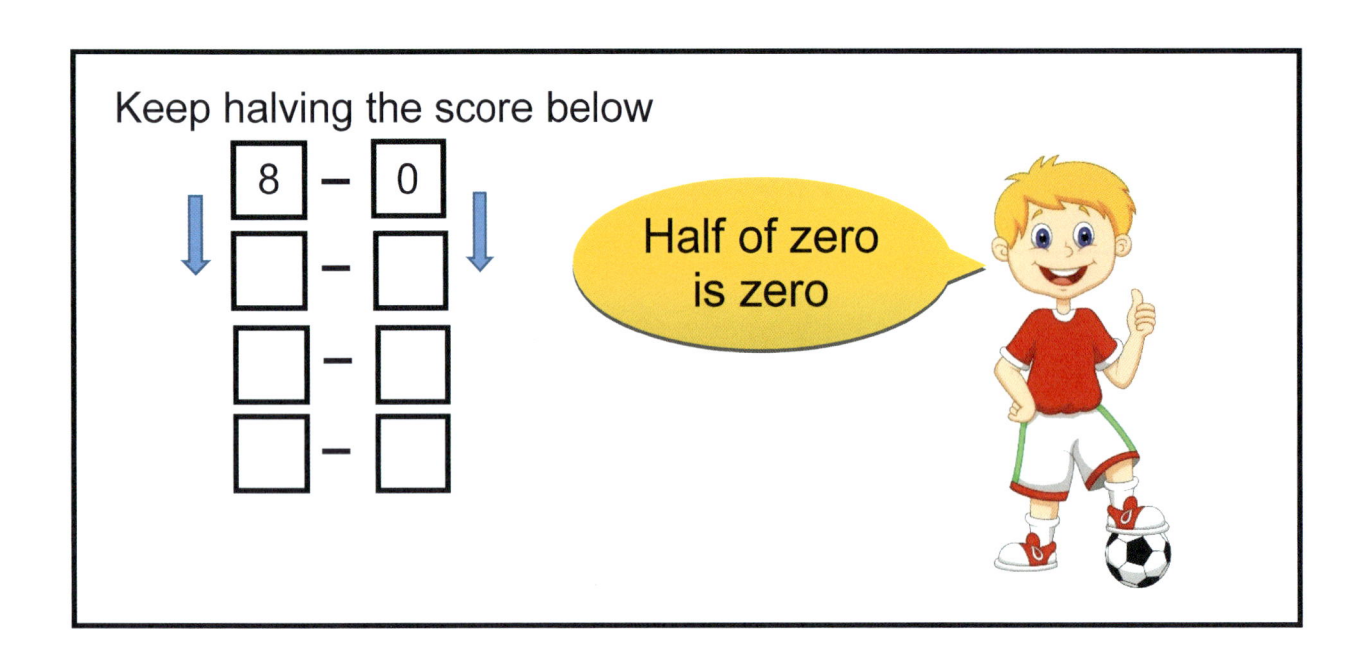

Below are the full-time scores in 4 matches. At half-time the scores were exactly half what the full-time scores were. Fill in the half-time scores below.

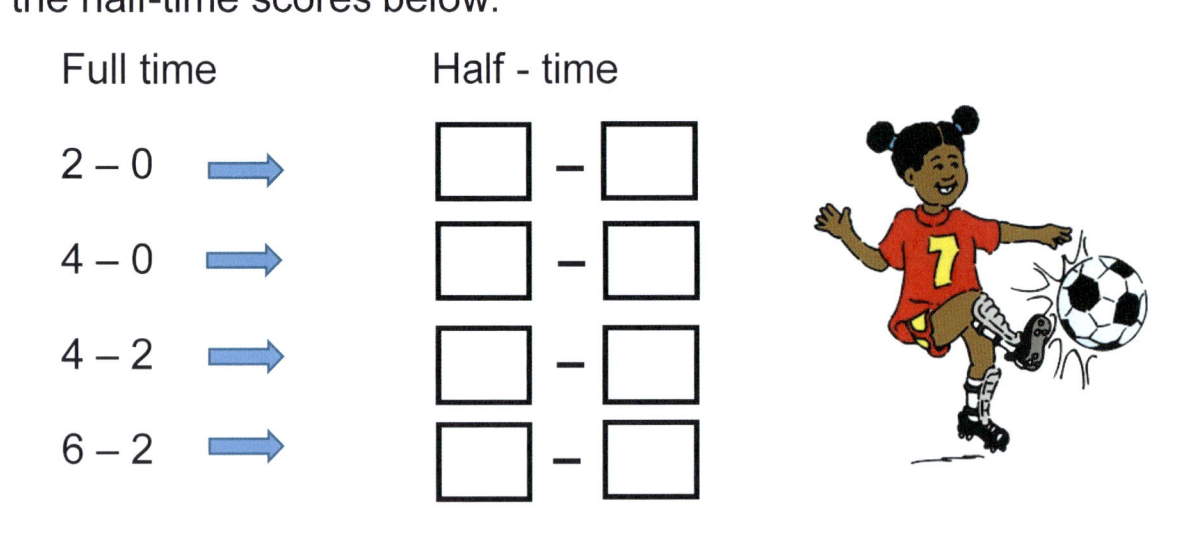

Full time   Half - time

2 – 0 →   ☐ – ☐

4 – 0 →   ☐ – ☐

4 – 2 →   ☐ – ☐

6 – 2 →   ☐ – ☐

Enter your score for this page: ☐ – ☐

How many teams play in a cup final?

Example: United v City

How many teams play in a semi-final?

Example: United v County

City v Town

How many teams play in a quarter final?

Example: Rovers v United

County v Argyle

City v Wanderers

Town v Albion

If 2 teams are playing each other in the cup, it's called a 'cup tie'

Enter your score for this page:

> If a cup tie consists of 2 matches, these are called the 'First Leg' and the 'Second Leg'

Sometimes in a **cup tie**, teams play each other twice, once at home and once away from home. When you add up each team's combined scores this is called the **aggregate score**.

	Home team		Away team
First Leg:	United	3 – 1	Town
Second Leg:	Town	2 – 3	United

How many goals did United score in total? ☐

How many goals did Town score in total? ☐

Complete the blanks below to find out the **aggregate score**:

_____ won by _____ goals to _____

Enter your score for this page: ☐ — ☐

The scores in the other semi-final are below:

	Home team		Away team
First Leg:	City	3 – 3	County
Second Leg:	County	2 – 1	City

City scored a total of ☐ goals

County scored a total of ☐ goals

Complete the blanks below to find out the aggregate score:

_____ won by _____ to _____

Enter your score for this page: ☐ – ☐

19

A football team consists of 11 players. As 1 player is always the goalkeeper, this leaves 10 outfield players.

Enter the number of defenders in this team ☐

Enter the number of midfielders in this team ☐

Enter the number of attackers in this team ☐

This is called a 4-3-3 formation.

Enter your score for this page: ☐ — ☐

Fill in the number of attackers in the 3 teams below to make sure they all have 10 outfield players.

Defenders | Midfielders | Attackers | | Total
| 4 | + | 4 | + | ☐ | = | 10 |

Defenders | Midfielders | Attackers | | Total
| 4 | + | 5 | + | ☐ | = | 10 |

Defenders | Midfielders | Attackers | | Total
| 4 | + | 3 | + | ☐ | = | 10 |

Number line

0   1   2   3   4   5   6   7   8   9   10

Enter your score for this page: ☐ — ☐

Fill in the number of midfielders in the 3 teams below to make sure they all have 10 players.

Defenders   Midfielders   Attackers   Total
  4   +   ☐   +   4   =   10

Defenders   Midfielders   Attackers   Total
  5   +   ☐   +   3   =   10

Defenders   Midfielders   Attackers   Total
  3   +   ☐   +   2   =   10

Number line

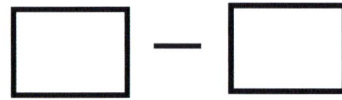

0   1   2   3   4   5   6   7   8   9   10

Enter your score for this page: ☐ — ☐

If a team's last 5 results were Win, Draw, Loss, Win, Draw, then this is written using the initials of the words = WDLWD

Your team's last 10 results were:
　　　DLWDWLWDLW

Enter the number of wins your team got ☐
Enter the number of draws your team got ☐
Enter the number of losses your team got ☐

Now check what the 3 numbers in the boxes add up to.

Number line
　　0　1　2　3　4　5　6　7　8　9　10

Enter your score for this page: ☐ — ☐

23

Keep track of the following match score as the goals go in! The first two are completed for you…

	Home	Away
Kick off	0 — 0
The home team quickly score 2 goals	2 — 0
The away team then pull a goal back	☐ — ☐
The away team get a penalty but miss it!	☐ — ☐
A home team player scores an **own goal**!	☐ — ☐

The ref blows the final whistle! Did you get the correct score?

If a home team player scores an own goal then he has scored a goal for the away team by accident!

How many of the six boxes above did you get right and wrong?
Enter your score for this page: ☐ — ☐

24

Keep track of the following match score as the goals go in! The first two are completed for you…

	Home	Away
KICK OFF	0 — 0
The away team scores after 10 minutes	0 — 1
The away team then double their lead	☐ — ☐
The home team's striker scores 2 goals!	☐ — ☐
HALF-TIME	
A home team player scores an own goal!	☐ — ☐
Free kick to the home team. He shoots. Goal!!	☐ — ☐
The home team get a penalty! Goal!!!!	☐ — ☐
FULL-TIME	

The referee blows the final whistle. Did you get the correct score?

Enter your score for this page: ☐ — ☐

United decide to buy 2 new players below. How much money have they spent in total?

Player	Cost
Gavin Kelly	£1 million
Mick Shearer	£1 million
Total Cost	£

Rovers decide to sell 2 players. How much money do they receive in total?

Player	Amount
Bob Robson	£2 million
Peter Smith	£3 million
Total amount	£

Enter your score for this page: ☐ — ☐

To score a goal you have to find a vertical route to the goal which is made up from **odd** numbers. Can you find the route?

6	2	9	1	1
1	8	3	4	3
2	6	8	5	7
6	3	7	9	9
7	9	2	1	5

Enter 1-0 if you got it right, or 0-1 if you didn't: ☐ — ☐

To score a goal this time you have to find a vertical route to the goal made up from even numbers. Can you find the route?

6	3	9	6	1
1	8	3	4	3
2	6	8	8	7
6	8	7	4	9
8	2	2	4	6

Enter your score for this page: ☐ – ☐

The first half of a football match lasts 45 minutes. Another way of looking at 45 is in tens and units:-

<u>Tens</u>   <u>Units</u>

40 + 5

The second half of a football match is also 45 minutes. Again this can be split into Tens and Units:-

<u>Tens</u>   <u>Units</u>

40 + 5

A match consists of the number of minutes in the first half + the number of minutes in the second half. How many is this in total?

Add the Tens for each half: 40 + 40 = ☐

Add the Units for each half: 5 + 5   = ☐

Now add the boxes to find out how long a match lasts ☐

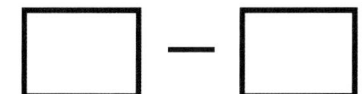

Enter your score for this page: ☐ — ☐

In an 11-a-side match, each team has 11 players. How many players are on the pitch in total:-

11
+ 11
___

___

Add the numbers downwards, starting with the ones nearest me, below the blue arrow

City have two strikers. At the end of the season John Smith had scored 25 goals and Gary Ward had scored 12 goals. How many have they scored in total?

John Smith   25
Gary Ward   + 12
___

___

Enter your score for this page: ☐ — ☐

Answers

Page

1 (a) 4, 6, 9 (b) 3, 8, 10

3 (a) 4   (b) 6

4 (a) 10 (b) 12

5 (a) 3, 2, 2 (b) 1, 2, 4

6 City 3 – 4 United

7 (a) Town 3 - 2 Argyle   (b) County 4 - 2 Albion

8 (a) United 3 – 2 Wanderers   (b) United 4 – 2 Albion

9 (a) 2, 3   (b) 6, 3

10 (a) 2-0, 4-0, 8-0   (b) 4-0, 6-0, 2-2, 2-4, 4-6

11] 2, 6, 3

12] 3, 4, 7

13] 8, 8, 7, 2

14] (a) Whole = 🙂, Half = 🌓, Quarter = 🌘   (b) ½ + 1 + ½ +1 = 3

15] 1=Odd, 4=Even, 8=Even, 5=Odd, 7=Odd, 9=Odd

16] (a) 4-0, 2-0, 1-0 (b) 1-0, 2-0, 2-1, 3-1

17] 2, 4, 8

18] 6, 3

19] 4, 5

20] 4, 3, 3

21] 2, 1, 3

22] 2, 2, 5

23] 4, 3, 3

24] 2-1, 2-1, 2-2

25] 0-2, 2-2, 2-3, 3-3, 4-3

26] (a) £2 million, (b) £5 million

27] Column 5

28] Column 4

29] 80, 10, 90

30] 22, 37

Other books by Adrian Lobley

The Football Maths Book Series

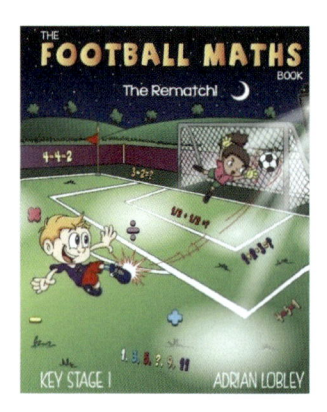

The Football Maths Book
- The Rematch!
(Book 2 in the series)
(Age 5-7)

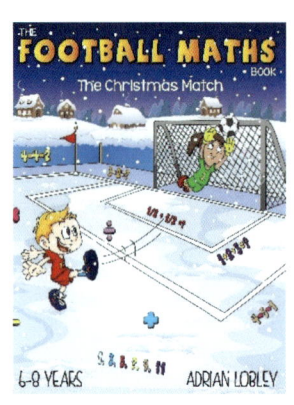

The Football Maths Book
- The Christmas Match
(Book 3 in the series)
(Age 6-8)

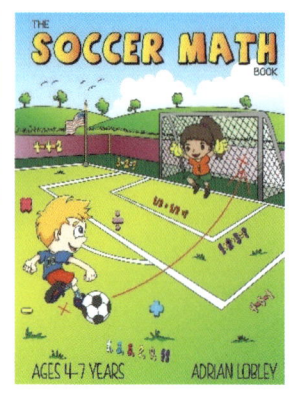

The Soccer Math Book
(US version of:
The Football Maths Book)
(Age 4-7)

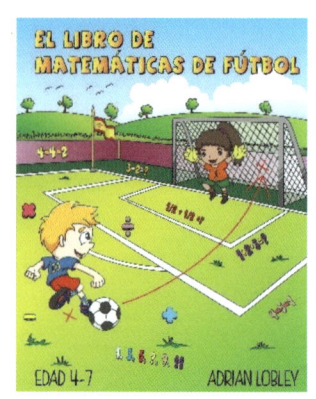

El libro de matemáticas de fútbol
(Spanish version of:
The Football Maths Book)
(Age 4-7)

The 'A Learn to Read Book' Series

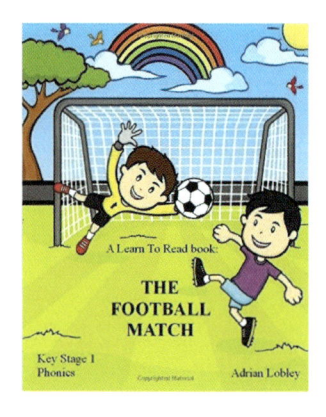

A Learn to Read Book:
The Football Match
(Age 4-5)

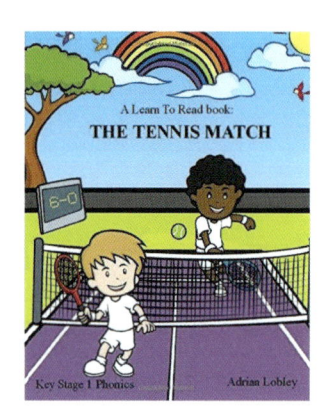

A Learn to Read Book:
The Tennis Match
(Age 4-5)

Printed in Poland
by Amazon Fulfillment
Poland Sp. z o.o., Wrocław

UP THE AVENUE

A Centenary Celebration of Bradford (Park Avenue)

**Malcolm Hartley
and Tim Clapham**

A SoccerData Publication
from Tony Brown

Published in Great Britain by Tony Brown,
4 Adrian Close, Beeston, Nottingham NG9 6FL.
Telephone 0115 973 6086. E-mail soccer@innotts.co.uk
First published 2007

© Malcolm Hartley & Tim Clapham 2007

All rights reserved. No part of this publication may be reproduced, stored in a retrieval system, or transmitted in any form, or by any means, electronic, mechanical, photocopying, recording or otherwise without the prior permission in writing of the Copyright holders, nor be otherwise circulated in any form or binding or cover other than in which it is published and without a similar condition including this condition being imposed on the subsequent publisher.

Cover design is by Bob Budd.

Photographs are from the authors' collections and permission has been sought for their use. Should we have overlooked a copyright please contact the publisher so that the mistake can be rectified in any future edition. Recent team groups and action shots are the copyright of Roy Sims.

Printed and bound by 4edge, Hockley, Essex
www.4edge.co.uk

ISBN 978-1905891-01-6

UP THE AVENUE!

THE BRADFORD (PARK AVENUE) CENTENARY BOOK

Contents

INTRODUCTION

AVENUE CHRONOLOGY
  You couldn't make it up
  Coming of Age – published 1928
  The Record Breakers
  The Lost Season
  When King George Reigned
  A Yorkshire KO
  New Decade, New Vision
  When Avenue Stood Alongside Chelsea
  End of the Road
  Phoenix

AVENUE MONTH BY MONTH

INTO THE UNKNOWN

CLOWN PRINCE REMEMBERED (BY TIM CLAPHAM)

PARK AVENUE AND ME (BY MALCOLM HARTLEY)

SHORTS

WHAT'S IN A NAME?

WHAT'S IN A DATE?

MAGAZINE MUSINGS

ALWAYS GOOD VALUE

THEY REPRESENTED BRADFORD

INTRODUCTION

(Unpromising career strangled at birth)

Derek, then Duncan, then Stan were all my companions at various standpoints of Park Avenue, and then came Hedley, known around Spinks's bar as Ted. He it was who, when I was in my early twenties, decided I might have a future in refereeing.

Actually that was part of his soft soap: he had approached everyone else he could think of but all had had the good sense to refuse to referee this friendly match at, I think, Queensbury.

"Anyway I can't do it because I don't have a whistle," was my last attempt to take my place among the band of cowards. "Don't worry," came the dispiriting reply, "we'll supply the whistle."

I had never refereed a match in my life and sleepless nights lay ahead. When the first offside dispute arose would I be stranded in the penalty area at the opposite end? What if a big, hefty pitbull of a full-back started to reduce the number of his opponents with ferocious fouls? Would I have the nerve to send him off? And if I did, would he go?

Supposing one of those knotty problems not covered by the laws of the game which are used for years afterwards at referees' quizzes cropped up? And was I even fit enough to stay somewhere near the play for 90 long minutes?

My knees were knocking as I approached the ground.

I was the only one disappointed when one of the teams did not turn up and the match was cancelled.

I wrote about this near miss in The Yorkshire Observer and was surprised when, three weeks later, the exact same words appeared in a national Sunday newspaper as a letter submitted by some cove called J. Brown of Helmsley Street, Bradford.

So my refereeing career never even began and I became an observer and a writer.

I met Tim Clapham in the middle 1980s and we teamed up to produce the first hardback book ever written on Bradford Park Avenue. By that time it was a look-back publication, recalling them as a decent average Championship team (then called the Second Division) who in 25 years slipped down and down, out of the Football League and then out of existence.

Our book was such a hit and inspired so much interest that the club was reborn and started the long climb back to respectability from lowly non-league circles.

We pay due tribute to all who worked so hard and spent so much in time and cash to haul Bradford Park Avenue to their current position. I have just been reading a survey in which supporters were asked to guess where their Premiership team would finish at the end of 2007-8. Not one of them contemplated relegation. This is the time of the year when optimism is rife. And with an enthusiastic new chief executive, Bradford's supporters too are looking ahead with renewed hope.

All good luck to them. In the meantime we can celebrate the centenary of the founding of the original club and this book is a miscellany of those 100 years with the focus mainly on the good times.

We place on record our sincere thanks to Mr Perry Austin-Clarke, Editor of Newsquest (Bradford) Ltd., publishers of the Telegraph & Argus and associated newspapers, for permission to reproduce part of a T&A page of 1966, a few lines from editions of 1958 and 1988 and other odds and ends. Our thanks, too, to Brian Hinchcliffe, Tony Farrell and Denis Clarebrough for the provision of photographs.

Malc Hartley (with Tim Clapham)
Bradford
August 2007

OPTIMISM. As mentioned above, August is the month of soccer optimism. Here Norman Brolls (from Third Lanark) scores in Bradford's public practice match of 1956, the fans' preview of the season in the days before half the team were injured in pre-season friendlies.

These games were arranged so that supporters could inspect the latest arrivals and guess which were other clubs' cast-offs and which might be genuine assets.

In August they all looked full of promise. By October some were looking a bit of a fool. By the end of the year several had been dropped.

I covered this game for The Yorkshire Observer and wrote that manager Bill Corkhill had "made some shrewd signings." That was not far out because among the newcomers were Charlie Atkinson, who went on to set a new club appearances record, and Cyril Robinson, holder of a Blackpool cup-winner's medal, who gave three seasons of service as a tough wing-half.

Mr Brolls was not marked down as impressive. He appeared in 11 fixtures, scored no goals and was last seen heading for Scarborough. And he wasn't the worst of the new faces.

In the stand was Peter Jackson, then manager of Bradford City, and his playing twin sons, David and Peter. A City fan quipped: "There are so many weaknesses at Avenue that it takes three to write them all down!"

Avenue finished the season two points clear of re-election.

YOU COULDN'T MAKE IT UP!

If the beginnings of Bradford Park Avenue FC were written down as fiction, readers would scoff at such high-flown fantasy. There were three factors that stretch credulity towards breaking point.
- First, the meeting to decide whether to exchange the rugby code for soccer voted to continue with rugby; but some crafty manoeuvring by club chairman Harry Briggs contrived to reverse the decision
- Second, having been turned down by the Football League, the club entered the Southern League. Who in his right mind would want a series of fixtures involving 400-mile return journeys in the days 51 years before the opening of the first motorway? Bradford's local derby was against Northampton - 130 miles away!
- And third, what on earth possessed members of the Southern League to agree to embracing a club 200 miles away in the frozen north, thereby committing every club to the expense, time and inconvenience of a lengthy journey?

There is a fourth remarkable aspect: Bradford reserves were placed in the North-Eastern League, so first and second teams played in competitions of almost geographical extremes.

Harry Briggs, whose personality and foresight brought soccer to Park Avenue, was a director of Rolls Royce, head of Brigella Mills - the worsted spinning mill founded by his grandfather in Little Horton, not far from Park Avenue - and had interests in Poland and in a large dyeworks near Leeds.

His life was devoted to business, cricket and football, he played for Bradford in the club's rugby days and he was chairman for more than 20 years. He supervised the removal of the club from Apperley Bridge to Park Avenue and as we have seen was responsible for the adoption of soccer despite strong opposition.

In 1910 the club was in debt for more than £4,000 and Mr Briggs cleared it. He also gave generously towards the maintenance of the county cricket ground and the bowling green pavilion was built at his expense.

It is interesting to note that when he died "The Yorkshire Observer" reported: "He was mortgagee of the Park Avenue estate and various efforts have been made to ensure that the estate shall remain a permanent home of first-class cricket and football. A complete success has not so far attended these efforts." What a shame it never did.

The cricket pavilion at Park Avenue

Mr Briggs bought Cottingley Hall and estate and lived in a mansion he built there called The Manor. He died on March 31, 1920, aged 56. His father, Mr Edward Briggs, died in 1898 - aged 56.

Harry Briggs did realise one dream when he saw Avenue among the elite, promoted to the First Division in 1914 and securing ninth place (in what is now the

Premiership) the following season before the Football League closed down for the remainder of the 1914-18 war.

He did not live to take the action he surely would have done to prevent Bradford from becoming the first club to suffer relegation in successive seasons (1921 and 1922).

They were always a power in the Third North, never out of the top five until they took the championship in 1928, and they were a decent Second Division outfit (third in 1929, fourth in 1930, fifth in 1934) for 20 years.

They lost their status in 1950, were required to beg for re-election for the first time in 1956, recovered to provide some exciting times in the first half of the 1960s and then collapsed alarmingly into oblivion.

The "new" Avenue (formed in 1988) progressed through the non-league pyramid until they were one league away from the Conference in 2004 but have slipped back to the Unibond Division One in which they last season finished fourth.

Tennis at Park Avenue, 1956

COMING OF AGE

The following pages are taken from a history of the club published in 1928. The author is unknown.

As the Bradford (Park Avenue) Association Football Club was born in the month of May 1907, it came of age at the completion of the 1927-8 season when emerging triumphant from the Northern Section of the Third Division to assume full League membership once more. This is an interesting fact which appears to have escaped notice at the time, but no less an important landmark in the history of a Club with a romantic, chequered and eventful past.

Although 21 years is but a comparatively brief space in the long reign of the Association game, it has to be asked if any other modern day club has had such varied and dramatic experiences as Bradford. These in some respects are unparalleled, as in the manner of the entry to competitive Association football, the rise to the heights of the First Division, and later plunge to Third League rank in the space of two seasons. The changes and upheavals embraced membership of no fewer than four senior competitions - the Southern League, the First and Second Divisions and the Northern Section of the Football League.

Looking back to the beginning, previous to 1907, save for one brief experiment with Association football, Park Avenue had been a recognised stronghold of the Rugby code, the Bradford Club having earned great fame in amateur and professional branches. But the dawning of the 20th century had been accompanied locally by a wider acceptance of the round ball game; in 1903 the Manningham Rugby Club gave place to the Bradford City Association Club, and there were those at Park Avenue who, despite the success of the Rugby team, believed that Association football would become the popular code of the future in the West Riding.

On April 15, 1907, a special meeting of the members was called to consider the situation and the Mayor of Bradford (Sir Arthur Godwin) occupied the chair. Three alternative proposals were put to the meeting. They were: Should the Northern Union game be continued at Park Avenue? Should the Club revert to the amateur code? Or should Association be adopted? The first question was answered in the affirmative on one vote, but a further test of views of the meeting resulted in a majority for Rugby Union football. It was thought that the future was clear, that the matter had been finally settled. It was, therefore, a surprise when it was announced a few days later that the members' meeting was *ultra vires* and the decision null and void, the influential Harry Briggs, who had a heavy financial interest in the Club, having taken counsel meanwhile with members of the committee and been in consultation with a solicitor. Although the announcement caused a storm, nothing could be done to prevent the ultimate adoption of the Association code early in May 1907, when it was decided to apply for admission to the Second Division of the Football League.

For that Division there were three vacancies and six applications made to the League Meeting on May 31. The Rev. James Leighton (affectionately known locally as the 'Sporting Parson') attended the meeting as Bradford's main spokesman to eloquently plead for the admission of his Club. But it was unavailing. To the consternation of all concerned Bradford were rejected. But then one of the Bradford party had an inspiration. It was to apply instantly to the Southern League, who were meeting the following day, for the place vacated by Fulham, they having been elected to the Second Division. The proposal - one of the most daring in the annals of football since it involved a huge outlay in travelling expenses - was acted upon and Bradford secured practically a unanimous vote in their election to the Southern League.

It should be mentioned that subsequently a suggestion was made for an amalgamation between Bradford and Bradford City, with Park Avenue as the ground for the combined club, this creating a bitter controversy before the proposal was defeated by the voting of the Valley Parade loyalists, who had formed a 'Defence Committee.' However, Bradford was established as an Association club with Fred Halliday as manager, Ernest Hoyle as secretary, and Edward Kinnear, formerly of Grimsby and The Wednesday, as trainer.

The first professional Association match played was at Park Avenue against Newcastle in the North Eastern League, the Bradford second team's fixtures having started first, on September 2, 1907. The Bradford side, made up of mainly first team players, won by 2-1 before an estimated crowd of 6,000. This was the forerunner to a greater victory five days later in the Southern League, when Reading were defeated at Elm Park by 3-1. Charles Carrick scored the first goal.

1907-08. Back: H O'Rourke, A Wood, AR Spence, SP Blott. Centre: JF Halliday (team manager), D McKie, C Milnes, CT Craig, J Christie, P Richards, A Robertson, E Kinnear (trainer). Front: A Ward, G Reid, H Finch, T Baddeley, D Mair, A Fisher, C Carrick.

Bradford certainly had an enjoyable experience in the Southern League in the course of a season which produced a dozen victories and provided some excellent football at Park Avenue, but, naturally, it was realised that first rank was unattainable while in membership of that subsidiary competition. With a progressive Chairman like Harry Briggs, there was always the wider sphere of the Football League in view, and yet it caused a sensation when in the spring of 1908 Bradford, Tottenham Hotspurs and Queens Park Rangers - three prominent clubs - resigned from the Southern League to apply for admission to the Second Division. Rangers, however, withdrew their application at the eleventh hour. The action of the other two incensed the Southern League authorities, for which reason the fate of the Bradford club certainly hung in the balance when the Rev. Leighton once again advocated their cause in support of the application to the Second Division. This time they were elected, the voting being as follows: Grimsby Town 32 votes, Chesterfield 23 and Bradford 20.

Bradford started their first Second Division campaign with a victory when Hull City were defeated by 1-0 at Park Avenue on September 1, 1908. A 12,000 crowd saw Alec Fraser score the Club's first Football League goal. It was in that season, one in which Bradford fully justified their inclusion in the Second Division by obtaining 32 points, that George Gillies succeeded Halliday as manager, and Tom Firth became trainer, he being followed shortly after by the long-serving Fred Chadwick.

The Bradford Club had hitherto been known as (The Incorporated) Bradford Cricket, Athletic and Football Club, however in August 1909 the Bradford (Park Avenue) Association Football Club Limited was established to manage the footballing side. The club leased the football ground, stands, dressing-rooms and offices to the company for 21 years, at an initial rent of £300 per annum. At the end of August 1909, 3,562 shares had been allotted to sixty applicants. 3,000 of these shares, or 84%, were owned by the Briggs family, 2,000 being in the name of chairman Harry Briggs. The largest shareholding apart from the Briggses' was 20 shares. It should be mentioned that 'Park Avenue' had been added to the Club's name in order to avoid any confusion with their neighbours across the city. The first directors were Mr A.H. Briggs (Chairman), Messrs. J. Brunt, H.T. Coates, H. Geldard, F. Lister, T.H. Marshall and A. Shepherd.

For three seasons Bradford met with average success and then, in 1911, Gillies resigned and Tom Maley was appointed manager. Maley had control of Manchester City previously and steered them to a Cup Final victory and he had sufficient confidence in his own judgment of players to give the assurance that he would pilot Bradford into the First Division. From Scotland he brought with him two of the best players the Club ever had in David Howie and George Halley, while he was instrumental in signing Herbert Dainty, who, with Halley and Jack Scott, formed what was Bradford's most famous halfback line. Even so, the team only occupied 13th place in season 1912-13, at the end of which Maley became secretary-manager, the position having been merged into one following the resignation of Ernest Hoyle.

1913-14, the team that won promotion. Back: Chadwick (trainer), Garry, Mavin, Drabble, Watson, Scott, Mr TE Maley (secretary), McCandless, Blackham, Bauchop. Front: Kivlichan, Little, Smith, Howie, Leavey.

Season 1913-14 saw Bradford gain promotion to the First Division, and it was made all the more memorable because it was necessary to beat Blackpool on the last day of the season by a substantial margin at Park Avenue to obtain a superior goal average to Arsenal. A score of 4-1 in Bradford's favour sufficed. After the final whistle a crowd of at least ten thousand filled the playing area and would not be satisfied until the players appeared and until Maley had made a speech. The side which featured in that historic match was: Drabble; Watson, Blackham; Garrie, Howie, Scott; Kivlichan, Little, Smith, McCandless and Leavey. Jimmy Bauchop was unable to play, but there was no doubt that the three inside forwards who regularly appeared for Bradford that season had much to do with the ultimate triumph, as instanced by the fact that Jimmy Smith, one of the Club's most intrepid centre-forwards, scored 25 goals, Tommy Little 24 and Bauchop 11. Alex Watson and Sam Blackham, of course, formed a most dependable rearguard, while Howie filled the centre-half position vacated by Dainty, who only appeared in seven games before returning to Scotland.

Thus Bradford in the comparatively brief period of seven seasons reached the charmed and select circle consisting of the most famous clubs in the land. They won two of their opening three matches, winning at Notts County, the side who had beaten them to the Second Division championship, before Europe was plunged into war. But the League decided to carry through the season's arrangements for 1914-15, and this gave Bradford the opportunity of thoroughly justifying their promotion. They completed the campaign with home victories against Manchester City and Bradford City to finish 9th and one point ahead of the men from Valley Parade.

The suspension of League football 'for the duration' found the majority of Bradford's team responding to the call of country and for the hostilities of European warfare in both the Navy and Army services. The supreme sacrifice was made by two: 2nd Lieut. Donald Bell, who was awarded the Victoria Cross, and Jimmy Smith. Their honoured memory was photographically perpetuated in the Recreation Room at Park Avenue. With these sad exceptions the team re-assembled after an interval of four years for the first post-war season with the addition of Bob Turnbull, a wartime international discovered on Teesside, and Walter Dickinson, left full-back. Subsequently David McLean, a Scottish international centre-forward, was signed from Sheffield Wednesday to make his first appearance on October 25, 1919.

Once again Bradford did not let themselves down finishing 11th, and their fifteen victories included a 6-2 win at Burnley and a 6-1 home thrashing of Aston Villa. They achieved this with a surprisingly small playing squad and were the premier Yorkshire club in a season which had been distinctly experimental following the war.

1921-22. Back: Lowson, Chadwick (trainer), Dickinson, Nicholson, Scattergood, Blackham, Maley (secretary/manager), McDonald. Front: Turnbull, Peel, G McLean, Howie, McCandless, Barnett

Through what was probably a strict sense of loyalty to their war-scarred and older players, who certainly had made an excellent resumption in First Division football besides going into the fourth round of the FA Cup, Bradford continued largely to pin their faith in them for the fateful season of 1920-1. But the hand of death was laid heavily upon Park Avenue by the Club being bereft of their chief patron and esteemed chairman, Harry Briggs, without whose generous support little enterprise could be projected. On the pitch everything appeared to go wrong, and Bradford ended the season at the bottom of the Division with just 24 points and were relegated. McLean's form was one of a few bright spots with the marksman netting half of the team's 44 League and Cup goals.

Despite some recruiting, Gerald Fell arriving from Barnsley in the February of 1922, and the promotion of local talent to the senior side, the decline could not be staved off, and Bradford made the amazing plunge into the Northern Section of the Third Division at the close of 1921-2. Second bottom, they had won more games at home than runners-up Stoke, but a shocking away record of two wins from 21 outings sealed their fate. From the heights to the depths in two seasons! Never had there been such a fall.

Would the Club survive the shock? The question was on everyone's lips and certainly a crisis had been reached. To the credit of those who had control of the affairs at the time, and in spite of a serious financial situation, the task of attempting to revive the Club's fortunes was bravely shouldered, and with the team receiving a further accession of strength from local and distant fields - Hubbert, Bradley, Hodgson, Wilcox, McCluggage, Brandon and Thompson all making their appearance in 1922-3 - Bradford from a stumbling beginning to their first Northern Section campaign climbed to the second position. Most of the League goals came from George McLean - younger brother of David - and Turnbull who claimed 20 apiece.

This hopeful bid for deliverance from the Northern Section was retarded somewhat in 1923-4, when the Club could only manage 5th place. But an invigorating influence had been brought to bear by the foundation of the Supporters' Club, which threw itself heart and soul into the restoration of the Club's status with financial and other assistance to the management, though in 1924-5 no further progress could be chronicled. By now there had been several changes on the management front with Peter O'Rourke and then David Howie having spells in the hot-seat in succession to the long-serving Maley who had departed in February 1924. A few months before leaving Park Avenue, Maley had made two excellent signings in Ken McDonald and Joe Myerscough, the former soon to be Bradford's goalscorer in chief.

The situation remained threatening and full of complexity when in 1925 Claude Ingram, a native of Bradford who had served his apprenticeship at Valley Parade, assumed the position of secretary-manager. Gifted with a genius for tackling financial problems, he at once applied it to the one at Park Avenue, and though it was necessary to transfer Turnbull and Andy McCluggage to Leeds United and Burnley respectively, the income derived from these transactions helped the Club over a difficult period and paved the way for fresh enterprise.

The sequel was the assembling of a side which in 1925-6 only missed promotion by a veritable hair's-breadth. It has been well-chronicled that the impediment of a mud-strewn goalmouth at Park Avenue prevented a goal being scored against Grimsby Town that would have made all the difference between success and narrow failure. At the end of the season Town clinched the championship and promotion having collected one more point than Bradford. McDonald beat Bauchop's 1914-15 record of 28 League goals with a return of 43 out of 101 racked up in the Northern Section.

Meanwhile changes had been occurring in the higher circles, the Chairmanship of the Board of Directors having been successively filled by Arthur Briggs, son of Harry, Richard Ingham, and then Stanley Waddilove, who introduced a restless energy and enterprise into the affairs of the Club, though in season 1926-7 Bradford had to be content with third place despite the team netting over 100 League goals once more. But this proved to be the springboard for a still bigger and triumphant season in 1927-8, which resulted in Bradford being restored to membership of the Second Division. The only dark cloud on the Club's horizon at this period was the death of Arthur Briggs, who, like his father, had given so generously to the Club.

1925-26. Back: Waddilove (director), Hubbert, Potts, Walker, Hodgson, Bailey. Seated: Quantrill, McLean, Fell, McDonald, Peel, Ingram (secretary/manager). Front: Myerscough, Taylor

    The summer interval had marked further notable recruiting by the signing of Bert Manderson, an Irish international right full-back, and also of a partner in Tommy Lloyd from Sunderland, and these two players, in addition to former Middlesbrough goalkeeper Jack Clough, who was to appear in every match during 1927-8, were destined to take a prominent part in the promotion season. Arthur Hawes was also acquired from Sunderland and Phil Cartwright joined from Middlesbrough, but he was unfortunately injured early in the season. This accident resulted in the trying of a young, immature local player - Herbert Davis - at outside-right, an experiment which proved to be a big success.

    Though Gerald Fell only appeared once during Bradford's championship-winning season his earlier service was not forgotten, nor that he, Harold Taylor and George McLean formed the surviving link between the promotion side and the one relegated six seasons previously. Bill Matthews, the big Welshman and centre-half who came to Park Avenue in 1925, shared with Clough the honour of being ever-present. Much of the credit of the Club's revival was rightly handed to Ingram who had been responsible for signing no fewer than sixteen of the most successful squad Park Avenue ever had.

    During the Club's triumphant campaign the team won 27 out of 42 matches in the Northern Section and finished eight points clear of runners-up Lincoln City. McDonald again headed the scoring chart with 29 League goals, while McLean scored 23 and Hawes 14 as the team netted 101 times for the third season in a row.

AUTHORS' POSTSCRIPT

This year of 2007 is the centenary not only of Park Avenue but also the Lord Mayoralty of Bradford.

A Bradford Daily Telegraph Date Book (published 1926) gives November 9, 1907, for the "opening of Park Avenue football pavilion."

It is mentioned in the article reproduced above that in April the Mayor of the city was Sir Arthur Godwin. In September he became the city's first Lord Mayor, the title being granted before his term of office ended in November.

We believed that Godwin Street must have been named after Sir Arthur but further research revealed that this major city centre thoroughfare was in fact named after his father, Alderman John Godwin, on the council 1863-8 and Mayor 1865-6, in recognition of his work on the Street Improvement Committee.

Incidentally Alderman John Godwin was at one time a partner in the wool firm of Milligan and Forbes, whose premises have long been occupied by the Telegraph & Argus. The first Mayor of Bradford in 1847 was Robert Milligan.

THE RECORD BREAKERS

If you fancy losing yourself in a dream world where Avenue seem to win almost every match and score shoals of goals, drink in the heady statistics of the 1920s.

From the aspects of points, goals and records, this was Bradford's happy decade. True, it began badly as they became the first club to be relegated in successive seasons. True most of it was spent in the Third Division North. But at whatever level you're playing, there, are teams out to stop you and Bradford's facts and figures for the period would be outstanding at any level.

Pre-season training, 1920s style, on the cricket ground at Park Avenue

The ground became Fortress Avenue! In seven seasons starting with 1922-3 Bradford lost only one home match per season, excepting 1926-7 when they didn't lose any.

In November 1927 they won their 25th consecutive home match in the Third North, needless to say a club record.

From March to August that year they scored four or more in six successive home games - four, six, five, five, four, six; average five every 90 minutes.

And from September 3, 1927 to March 1928 they were unbeaten in 16 successive away matches.

On September 25, 1925, they recorded their biggest-ever victory in the Football League, 8-0 at home to Walsall (Joe Myerscough, George McLean, Ken McDonald and Harold Peel two each, Alf Quantrill none.)

In 1927-8 Bradford scored 101 goals for the third season in succession.

In 1925-6 centre-forward Ken McDonald set up a club record which stood for 40 years by netting 43 times and was still not the Third North's top scorer. That distinction went to Jimmy Cookson who notched 44 for Chesterfield in what was at the time a new league record.

It is a surprise to find that the prolific McDonald despite heading Avenue's goalscoring list four times and in those seasons netting 118 goals, was never the chief marksman in the division.

His career total of 174 in 214 games gave him a goals-per-game average of 0.81 - and that has been bettered by only nine players in history. In fact the great Dixie Dean is one place in front of him with 0.86. At the top is Derek Dooley (Sheffield Wednesday - see "A Yorkshire Knock-out") with 64 from his 63-match career. Fourth, incidentally, is Brian Clough with 251 in 274 for an average of 0.91.

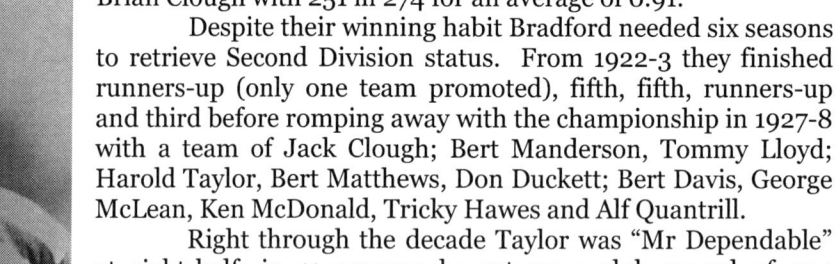

Despite their winning habit Bradford needed six seasons to retrieve Second Division status. From 1922-3 they finished runners-up (only one team promoted), fifth, fifth, runners-up and third before romping away with the championship in 1927-8 with a team of Jack Clough; Bert Manderson, Tommy Lloyd; Harold Taylor, Bert Matthews, Don Duckett; Bert Davis, George McLean, Ken McDonald, Tricky Hawes and Alf Quantrill.

Right through the decade Taylor was "Mr Dependable" at right-half: in 11 seasons he set up a club record of 334 appearances (later overtaken by Charlie Atkinson) and cup record of 25.

Harold Taylor

George McLean was a Scottish diamond of an inside-forward who could pass shrewdly, shoot fiercely, read the game and bring the best out of his colleagues. He left for Huddersfield Town where it was widely accepted that when he suffered a broken leg at Easter 1934 it ended Town's First Division championship hopes. They led Arsenal on goal average but after the Scot's misfortune (a "collision" with Sam Cowan) they lost three of the next four and ended runners-up. McLean was leading scorer with 18 and would have been Town's Player of the Year had such a trophy been available.

Quantrill, a winger of speed and intelligence, came with a Derby County-Preston pedigree and four England caps.

At centre-half Bill Matthews already had a Third Division championship medal, earned with Bristol City in 1922-3. At Wrexham he had been regarded as the most attractive centre-half in the Northern Section. Tall and constructive, he had survived the Battle of the Somme to earn three Welsh caps, one of them while at

Alf Quantrill in action

Bradford against Ireland in February 1926. He was a keen cyclist until deep into his 70s.

In 1928-9 Bradford finished third in the Second Division and in 1929-30 they ended fourth. Derring-do on the pitch was reflected on the terraces - for four consecutive seasons Bradford had the highest average crowd in the Northern section (8,050 in 1924-5, followed by 12,843, 10,507 and in the championship season 13,514).

1929-30. Back: Smith, Geldard, Dinsdale, McCandless, Matthews, Scott, Kilcar, Murphy, Lloyd. Next to back: Bartlett (assistant trainer), Nuttall (trainer), Cooke, Atherton, Millership, Moody, Clough, Elwood, Godfrey, Sullivan, Leonard, Ingram (secretary/manager). Seated: Buckley, Reid, McLean, Davis, Cookson, Parrish, Rhodes, Parris, Dickinson. Front: Quantrill, Taylor

Bradford made the front cover of the weekly "Sports Budget" in April 1933. From the left, Bedford, Elwood, Lloyd and Parris.

17

THE LOST SEASON: 1939-40

The 1939-40 season began with Jubilee matches to raise money for a benevolent fund set up to mark 50 years of the Football League. Similar games had been arranged before the start of 1938-9.

Avenue opened with a Saturday evening match (kick-off 6.30) at home to City on the day Eccleshill won the Priestley Cup for the first time, beating Spen Victoria by nine wickets on the other side of the football club's main stand. It was an inauspicious portent when both Jack Wesley and Billy Martin missed penalties, though these two and Bill Hallard gave them a 3-0 half-time lead, reduced in the second half by Hastie and Colquhoun. The attendance was 4,843.

There was concern that right-back Urbon Lindley had broken a leg near the end but it turned out to be no worse than severe bruising and it opened the way for the first appearance of a teenager called Jimmy Stephen.

The first matches of the season presented something new to followers - every team for the first time had numbers on their shirts. Bradford began at Chesterfield and were soon feeling aggrieved when a shot from centre-forward Fred Smith was cleared off the line by Kidd. They felt it was well over but Harry Nattrass (cup final referee of 1936) disagreed. After ten minutes Les Miller crossed for Tommy Lyon to head Chesterfield ahead and two minutes later South African Dudley Milligan doubled the lead after Lyon had confused defenders by jumping over the ball. The home side would have had more but for Chick Farr who was in brilliant form. Bradford's most dangerous forward was winger Jack Hughes who was returning to the ground of his most recent club. Bob Danskin, having undergone an uncertain first half against the robust Milligan, eventually put the clamp on his activities.

Jimmy Stephen

Six changes were made for the Wednesday visit of Luton Town with 17-year-old Stephen making his debut alongside another young back in Ron Hepworth, who was 20. It was reported that Stephen made a good debut but he was probably unhappy in his own mind about events because on the half-hour he took the ball almost out of Farr's hands, failed to clear and Hugh Billington shot in from an angle. And with four minutes to the final whistle Stephen deflected Reg Stockill's centre into his own net. "If nothing else Farr's goalmouth wanderings amused some people," said local writer George Thompson. The crowd for the first home game of the season numbered only 7,319. War clouds were hanging overhead.

On September 2 Bradford received Millwall - and former Avenue inside-left Don Barker - in what turned out to be the last Football League match for seven years. Hallard and Eddie Watson (from Huddersfield) "brought some method into the attack" and Tommy McGarry scored Bradford's first goal of the season which gave them a half-time lead. Then Beattie equalised, Watson put Bradford back in front (69 mins) but Richardson made it 2-2 (77 mins). Hepworth played with cool assurance but Stephen had a hard time against Barker and outside-left Reg Smith, who had twice been selected for England the previous season.

Luton were Second Division leaders. Avenue found only Fulham and Burnley below them on goal average.

Next day we were at war with Germany.

18

WHEN KING GEORGE REIGNED

Thursday September 11, 1947. In Oscar Hammerstein's words to the Richard Rodgers song, "Oh what a beautiful morning, oh what a beautiful day!"

That's how it seemed to Avenue supporters that day when we could look at, disbelieve, pinch ourselves, look again, and see the Second Division league table with Bradford at the top - played six, won six, drawn none, lost none, goals for 18, goals against three; 12 points.

It was the club's best-ever start. At the time, anyway. We can argue about this in a minute. But at that moment it was First Division (Premiership these days) here we come!

Only once previously had Bradford won so many as five consecutive games outside the Third Division. That was in 1913 and those five wins did actually push them towards promotion to the top flight.

In 1947 unbeaten Avenue were keeping pace with Arsenal, whose record at the top of the First Division was played six, won six, goals for, 19; goals against five; 12 points. The significance of this would be seen later in the season.

Was it really the club's best-ever start? Many will argue for 1964-5 because after beating Darlington 3-1 at home on October 3 Bradford were top of Division Four with six wins and six draws from their opening 12 fixtures, their 18 points keeping them at the top two ahead of Tranmere and Doncaster.

But that was in the Fourth Division. And remember when Carlisle United won their first three matches in the First Division in 1974-5? A reproduction of the league table showing Carlisle as the top team in England hung in Brunton Park for years afterwards. True, they were bottom at the season's end but no one could deprive the Cumbrians of their hour of glory - as magical as snow before the footprints!

For me, it was much the same with Avenue in 1947 - just 40 years after the club had been formed.

What has been generally overlooked about that short but glittering spell in the club's history is that they were captained by George Wilkins, father of sons who figured later in the Football League, most notably Ray, of Chelsea, Manchester United and England. And Dean, current manager of Brighton.

George had been signed from Brentford in February 1947. A balding inside-right, he was a constructive master, the tactical brain of the team and a leader whose experience and expertise was respected by his colleagues.

He was ably abetted by left-half Bill Layton, another methodical player who packed a thunderous shot in his boots. In the first match against West Ham they combined to make the team's first goal of the season after eight minutes when Layton's cross-field ball to Wilkins was turned into a low pass just right for Harry McIlvenny to drive past Ernie Gregory.

The visit to Nottingham to take on Forest the following Wednesday brought the second victory - and here's something for the record-keepers. The papers credited Jackie Smith with both goals but the Yorkshire Sports then corrected this, an amendment previously overlooked, by stating that the second was scored by McIlvenny.

Wilkins was superb at Trent Bridge. "He was the schemer-in-chief, his crafty distribution frequently splitting Forest's defence," reported The Yorkshire Observer. And manager Fred Emery said: "After the first ten minutes it became one of the few matches I ever remember when I was left without the slightest uncomfortable moment about what the result would be."

Chesterfield came to town on Saturday August 30 and were vanquished when a picture cross-field pass from Wilkins enabled Billy Elliott to centre for Smith to close in and leave Ray Middleton blinking as he crashed home the winning goal.

In the return against Nottingham Forest, Bradford won 3-1 with Wilkins "applying the touches of craft and leadership which made others want to respond with equal zest."

Millwall were our visitors on Saturday September 6 and were put to the sword 4-0. Johnny Downie notched two before half-time, Arthur Farrell potted a penalty after Elliott had been brought down and Layton crowned a silky-smooth left-wing move with a shining shot that dazzled goalkeeper Jim Purdie.

Victims of the sixth in succession were Doncaster Rovers as Bradford hit four more without reply and the third, scored by George Wilkins, brought the biggest cheer of the season from Avenue's largest crowd of 18,942.

So Bradford, with 12 points, led the table from West Brom (11) and four clubs on eight, including Leeds United.

It was asking a lot for a seventh straight win because the next fixture took Avenue to White Hart Lane. They held Spurs to a goalless first half but after that Les Horsman missed a fierce low cross from Les Stevens but Len Duquemin did not, and then "the Duke" headed Spurs further ahead from a Stevens corner. Another Stevens corner brought a third to home star Jimmy Jordan, an inside-right who was one of England's early exports when he signed for Juventus in August 1948.

Horsman had gone upfield to centre-forward at 0-2, Layton moving to centre-half, and near the end he saw a goal-bound header handled off the line by a defender for Farrell to reduce the margin to 3-1 from the spot.

No disgrace in that, but the result from the following Thursday's trip to Doncaster was a shock - a 3-0 defeat after Wilkins had been injured in the first few minutes.

Avenue extended their 100% home record by seeing off Sheffield Wednesday 2-0, giving them a home goal haul of 17-2 from five outings.

Nicholls, the Bradford goalie, misses and Duquemin, Spurs' centre-forward, gets ready to score.

Chick Farr retrieved the green jersey in this match, Jim Nicholls having deputised as he completed his recovery from a broken arm suffered towards the end of 1946-7, and starred in the next match, away to Cardiff. But for his display of heroics Cardiff's margin would have been more pronounced than 1-0 - a goal scored just eight minutes from the end.

That was about the end of Avenue's thoughts about promotion. One win and a draw from nine games dropped them to 13th. But during this disappointing sag there was one piece of happy news - right-back Jimmy Stephen was chosen for Scotland against Wales at Hampden, becoming the only Scot to be given full international status while with the club (though he had played in five war-time internationals for his country).

The next cheerful occasion was the visit of leaders West Bromwich Albion on November 29. The previous Wednesday Bradford had made an enterprising double signing from Leeds United of forwards George Ainsley and Gerry Henry and Ainsley immediately made his mark with two goals in a 2-1 triumph. He was great in the air and thoughtful with his groundwork. On the same day Arsenal suffered their first defeat in the First Division, 1-0 at Derby.

When Bradford drew their next match at Barnsley it could be regarded as the perfect result. At the final whistle Bradford had 20 points from 20 matches and were tenth, Barnsley 20 points from 20 matches and stood eleventh!

Ainsley and Henry (2) vanquished Plymouth Argyle at Avenue on December 13 and only Newcastle (41) had scored more times in the division than Bradford (38), while no one matched our lads' 28 at home.

Nottingham Forest, having noted Wilkins's fine football against them in early season days, now came in with an offer of £7,500 and the man who led Bradford to the top left for the East Midlands.

Top scorer Johnny Downie was released from his work as a Bevin Boy (sent down the mines to produce much-needed coal under a scheme introduced by Minister of Labour Ernest Bevin) but Stephen missed matches because he was in the RAF.

The cup draw sent Avenue to Highbury to face First Division giants Arsenal with whom they had kept pace over the first six matches. And the Second Division mid-tablers pulled off one of the most outstanding results in their history. Captain Ronnie Greenwood - later manager of England - was man of the match while Billy Elliott - later to play for England - scored the only goal after 36 minutes and gave ageing international right back George Male a hard afternoon. Arsenal went on to win the league championship.

Avenue followed up this historic triumph with another happy visit to the metropolis, beating Millwall at The Den by the only goal. But their next trip south had the opposite outcome. Drawn against Southern Leaguers Colchester United in the fourth round of the cup, they shot from the top of the glory scale to the bottom and lost 3-2. Training on oysters supplied by the local fishery board, the Essex club were already giant-killers having knocked out First Division Huddersfield Town, but another top flight club, Blackpool, took care of them in the fifth round.

It was a month before Bradford recovered sufficiently to win again but it was perhaps worth waiting for - a very welcome 3-1 margin at home to Leeds United before a crowd of 21,040. It was a joy day for George Ainsley who collected a hat-trick against his recent employers.

And there was a thrilling Easter when Bury were battered 4-0 at Gigg Lane and then 5-3 at Park Avenue, Bradford leading 5-0 after 50 minutes. Note that the only time Avenue had previously scored more than nine against the same opponents in the same season was against Manchester United in 1933-4 (6-1 at home, 4-0 away).

It was the last fling of a season that fizzled out with anticipated defeats against Newcastle (promoted), Birmingham (champions) and away to West Bromwich (6-0, heaviest reverse of the campaign).

Johnny Downie was top scorer with 19 while Ainsley bagged 13 in 18 appearances. The team were equal eleventh on points but inferior goal average dropped them to 14th in the final table.

HUGE CUP CROWDS

The following season, 1948-49, also got off to a bright start. Cardiff were caned 3-0 in, unusually for the opening day, persistent rain, and there was a 3-2 victory at Blackburn in a remarkable match of three penalties, all to Rovers. Campbell shot wide from the first and then Gray scored from the other two. How many teams concede three spot kicks and still win?

A lone goal defeat away to Queen's Park Rangers left Bradford third behind Fulham and Rangers and they then completed the double over Blackburn when they themselves were awarded a penalty from which Gerry Henry gave them the lead.

Avenue moved up to joint leaders with Southampton after lashing Luton 4-1 - four wins from the opening five - but the long trail to Plymouth proved fruitless and a 2-0 defeat followed at Coventry.

Bradford had fallen to 12th when they travelled to Grimsby on October 2 and won 3-0. Johnny Downie had a great match and scored twice. The

October 1948 at White Hart Lane. Farrell clears from Len Duquemin, the Spurs' centre-forward.

Mariners had a reputation for their hospitality, all opponents and the officials always being presented with parcels of fish to take home. One of the Bradford players astounded everyone else on the coach home by taking his fish and eating it - raw!

The team had lost three in a row when leaders West Bromwich Albion came to Avenue on November 20. Pugnacious Billy Elliott was moved from the left wing to left-half and did so well that he kept his new position for the rest of the season. Bradford rocked the top dogs 4-1 and followed up by winning 3-1 at Chesterfield and then returned with an extraordinary margin of 6-3 from Lincoln which not only pulled them to fifth in the table but left them leading scorers in the section with 42 goals from 20 matches.

Three defeats and a goalless draw was poor preparation for the cup. A year ago the draw had given them an away tie against the First Division leaders (Arsenal, who were beaten 1-0) and now they had to travel to the club standing second in the First Division - Newcastle United, jousting for the lead with Portsmouth.

Yet once again Bradford shocked the football world, goals from Downie and Harry McIlvenny taking them through to the fourth round again. McIlvenny put on perhaps his best display for the club but man-of-the-match honours went to centre-half Les Horsman for blotting out England centre-forward Jackie Milburn.

The players set off for the Newcastle cup-tie, January 1949. From left; Arthur Farrell, Jimmy Stephen, Les Horsman, Harry McIlvenny, Chick Farr, Billy Elliott, Roy White, Billy Deplidge, Johnny Downie, Alec Glover, George Ainsley, Alan Ure (trainer)

Next Saturday the boys in red, amber and black travelled to Luton and became the first to take two points from Kenilworth Road through a goal by Gerry Henry. Dick Williamson's love of alliteration found full flow as he referred to another "form-flouting feat."

The following week Bradford led Coventry 2-1 at half-time and the remainder of the contest was memorable for a wonder display by visiting goalkeeper Alf Wood. He flung himself at shots from all angles and repelled the lot, especially some blockbusters from Henry.

Then it was cup week again. Amazingly, having given Bradford away ties against the First Division leaders in 1948 (Arsenal) and a year later the second-placed top flight club (Newcastle), the draw now made them visit the third-placed club among the elite! This was Manchester United, at the time playing at Maine Road, home of Manchester City, because of war damage at Old Trafford.

Could Avenue pull off a hat-trick of triumphs against the giants? Well, they nearly did. The biggest crowd before which they ever played, 82,771, saw them take the lead when Henry headed in from a Deplidge corner for a lead they held at half-time.

Five minutes after the turn, however, Mitten equalised and although Jack Rowley (later to become an Avenue manager) hit the post there were no further goals, even in extra time, and Matt Busby's men had to come to Bradford for a replay.

This was Bradford's first all-ticket match but on a frosty, murky day it turned into a tetchy encounter. United, playing in blue shirts, produced the better football and made more chances but through a Farrell penalty for hands Avenue drew 1-1. The afternoon was marred, however, when Harry McIlvenny suffered a broken leg in extra time.

The second replay brought a decisive end to the tie. It was played only 48 hours later on the Monday and this time United's class was emphasised in the score. Avenue held it to 0-0 for 27 minutes and a single goal at half-time but after that the roof fell in and but for some magnificent saves by Chick Farr the margin would have been worse than 5-0.

Nevertheless those cup-ties in two seasons against First Division big boys produced two away wins, two draws and only one defeat, with the following remarkable attendance figures:

v Arsenal 47,738
v Newcastle United 47,196
v Manchester United 82,771
v Manchester United 29,092
v Manchester United 70,434
Total: 277,231, average 55,446.

Johnny Downie benefited from the battle with United because it brought his form to the eyes of Matt Busby who found £18,000 to add him to his side on March 2. He was subsequently a member of the Manchester United team that won the First Division title in 1951-2.

His last match in Avenue colours was on February 26 at home to Grimsby and it was one of those games that send supporters wild with frustration. No goals had been scored as the second half melted away and wave after wave of Avenue raids failed to reach the net. Then with three minutes left, a long clearance found Grimsby's ace marksman Tommy Briggs, in the centre circle. With nearly all the home team committed to attack he had a clear run for goal and took the chance to steal the winner. Knifed in the last reel!

February 1949, an FA Cup tie at Park Avenue. Farr punches clear from Burke of Manchester United. Horsman watches closely.

Or, as Dick Williamson had it in his own inimitable and sometimes obscure way: "There is no escape from the conclusion that something is radically wrong with a forward line whose accurate marksmanship so closely approximates to the irreducible minimum as makes no matter, which is what Bradford's attack perpetrated here."

On March 12 came Leicester City who scored a memorable goal in a fine match which ended 3-3. Avenue were two up when Maldwyn Griffiths, City's clever Welsh international outside-right, tricked Farrell, beat Horsman and then cut the ball back. Don Revie stormed up from inside-right and smashed the ball at full tilt from 30 yards into the postage stamp corner.

Bradford made it 3-1 on the hour but Jack Lee (later capped by England) and Revie again three minutes from time earned the visitors their point. Those who had seen the teams' earlier meeting at Filbert Street in October described it as thrilling as any game involving Bradford since the war and that, too, ended in a draw (2-2).

On a miserably wet Monday evening (April 4) leaders Southampton were beaten more comprehensively than the 2-0 margin indicates. Gerry Henry, stocky and combative inside-right, was outstanding and the following Saturday he was again in top form with a hat-trick which helped bury Bury 4-1.

They did not know it but that victory in the 36th match was the last of the season. A sorry Easter saw a double conceded to Nottingham Forest and a dreadful 7-1 walloping at West Bromwich.

On Wednesday May 4 bottom-of-the-table Lincoln (beaten 6-3 at Sincil Bank, remember) came to Avenue and won 3-0 with Jock Dodds, their big rumbustious centre-forward, outstanding. Near the end we had Parr v Farr - a penalty which Lincoln's inside-left fired against the post.

Nowadays it is no longer unusual to find a goalkeeper up in the opposition's penalty area in the last minute of a game, hoping his height will bring about a late equaliser or winner, but in 1949 it was unheard of unless you happened to support Bradford and saw Chick Farr.

Chick was a great character who was known occasionally to come out and take a throw-in. But he went Farr-ther than usual in the last minute of the last match at home to Sheffield Wednesday when at 1-1 he dribbled half the length of the field in seeking to set up a winner. The attempt failed but at least he made it back to his own goal before Wednesday could take play back into Avenue's half.

Ninth after the victory at Bury, Bradford fell to 17th in the final table because of that disappointing stretch of two points from the last possible twelve.

February 1949: In the FA Cup second replay at Maine Road, (above) Farr makes a fine save with Stephen and Farrell in attendance, and (right) Rowley of Manchester United is foiled when Farr in the Bradford goal punches clear.

25

Action from a cup tie at Millwall, 1950. Mitch Downie in the Bradford goal looks back as Neary of Millwall (arms outstreched) heads a goal.

In the replay with Millwall at Park Avenue, Crosbie leaps for the ball.

A YORKSHIRE KNOCK-OUT: 1951-52

Bradford were seventh in the Third North when in November 1951 the FA Cup trail was opening to league clubs and the draw sent them to York, six places below them.

Bob Crosbie gave Avenue a half-time lead but after the break York piled on painful pressure and only the resilience of goalkeeper Mitch Downie and defenders Les Horsman and Frank Hindle kept them at bay until Alf Patrick headed a free kick equaliser.

The replay also ended 1-1 (after extra time) but when the teams met for a third time at Elland Road Avenue romped into the next round 4-0 (Haines 2, Turner, Crosbie).

They had had ample incentive to shake off York because the draw had pitted the winners against Bradford City at home. So it was a local derby in the second round and 24,430 made their way to Park Avenue to dispute proceedings verbally.

Avenue won a fair-minded match 3-2 with two goals from Phil Turner and a header by Terry Lyons from an Alex Wright centre against City's two from Millar and Greenhoff

Turner, Haines and Jeff Suddards - whose well-placed free kick gave Turner his first - were the men who mattered for the home side. Little Polly Ward (who later crossed the city) at inside left worried the home defence.

A third round draw against one of the top clubs - Manchester United, Portsmouth or Newcastle - might have been welcomed but instead Bradford were given a home tie against Sheffield Wednesday, second in Division Two, and the talk of football because of the scoring exploits of big, awkward Derek Dooley, who had hit two or more in six successive matches in the autumn and notched a total of 28 in 16 league matches.

A tough day ahead for Les Horsman it seemed. But Les had mastered England international Jackie Milburn at Newcastle in the cup only three seasons previously and he countered the raiding red-head with enthusiasm and pragmatic defensive play. True, Dooley's name appeared on the score-sheet after only five minutes but after that he was well subdued.

And Phil Turner - a brace against City, remember - was twice more on the mark to put Bradford through. The "Empire News" observed: "Those old Tottenham touches introduced by Bradford manager Vic Buckingham were evident in the well spread passes of Haines and Turner."

You may have noticed by now that all Bradford's cup opponents were Yorkshire teams so was anyone surprised when the fourth round draw again kept them in the county with a visit to Leeds United?

This match was watched by 50,645 who saw two United defenders successfully brought into attack. After 31 minutes Roy Kirk, normally a half-back but now on the right wing, centred for Jim Milburn, left-back masquerading as a centre-forward, to open the scoring. In the second half Leeds made it 2-0 following another Kirk centre.

Up front the Avenue forwards foundered on the centre-half play of 20-year-old John Charles, though the inside forwards, Turner and Haines, again made great efforts.

Looking back on that team of the early 1950s one wonders why they were not more prominent in the promotion struggle.

They had players of the calibre of Jeff Suddards, a ridiculously constructive full-back by Third North standards, the indomitable Frank Hindle, the ebullient Les Horsman at centre-half and Charlie Currie at right-half who had won every available honour in Northern Ireland with Belfast Celtic and representative honours with the Irish League.

And partnering international Jack Haines (one cap, two goals) at inside forward was Phil Turner. He had been in Bill Shankly's Carlisle United team which had a day of glory in 1951 when they held Arsenal to a goalless draw at Highbury in the third round of the cup. And they had come close to an exciting victory. The 'Evening Standard" reported: "Twenty minutes after the restart Carlisle nearly scored. Turner hit a beauty on the bounce but was left to throw up his hands when Platt made a flying save against all the odds."

Phil made a hit at Avenue after coming down from Cumberland by scoring 14 in his first 16 outings, proving highly mobile and a danger with both head and feet.

Against Oldham (December 1) it was reported: "Bradford's attack profited vastly from the inspiring example set by Turner, the most spectacular forward in the game." It turned out to be Phil's best-ever season and he finished top scorer with 22 goals in 40 league outings plus five in four cup-ties. After leaving Bradford he turned out for Scunthorpe and Accrington before returning to his first league club, Chester. And he was still playing football in some local league in his 50s.

Bradford finished 1951-2 in eighth place.

1958: New manager Walter Galbraith (third left) meets his players.

A cup tie at Chelsea in January 1960. Brabrook (right) heads Chelsea's third past Harry Hough while Lawton watches.

NEW DECADE, NEW VISION

1960-1 was a vintage season in the annals of English football.

Streamlined Spurs became the first modern team to complete the double with players of wonderful cohesion and fluency under Danny Blanchflower. England scored 45 goals in nine internationals and clobbered the Scots 9-2. Peterborough broke the league scoring record in their first Football League season (134). Ipswich staggered everyone by winning the Second Division title only 23 years after admission to the league. For the first time a league match was televised live. The League Cup was introduced. And Bradford won promotion!

They began by winning their first away match for the first time in ten years. Jock Buchanan worried Workington to bits. He scored twice and his subtle promptings enabled Ian Gibson to enjoy his day on the left wing.

Misfortune struck two minutes into the first home game, against Chester. Quicksilver little outside-left Ray Byrom, who had not missed a match the previous season, suffered a double break in his leg and was ruled out for the season. It happened on a sunny August evening and was the first game his wife had seen him play. My notes for the match show that, including a hold-up of three minutes while the unlucky Byrom received attention, the first half ran for 53 minutes.

However, the remaining ten (substitutes then unknown in the Football League) won with another Buchanan goal, with Gibson again shining, skipper Charlie Atkinson working as if his life depended on the result and Wattie Dick and Joe Baillie adding a large measure of tactical skill.

As the Rome Olympics opened, 19-year-old amateur Trevor Lightbown was given Byrom's place and Oldham were sent back across the Pennines on the wrong side of a 5-1 pasting.

Yorkshire (Stott, Bolus, Padgett, Close, Taylor, Illy, Trueman, Don Wilson, Binks, Cowan and Vic Wilson, the county's first professional captain of the century) overcame Worcestershire to retain the county cricket championship and as Avenue's encouraging start faltered with two away defeats manager Walter Galbraith signed tiny tricky Jimmy Anders from Buxton for the No. 11 spot.

It was Anders's second spell at Park Avenue and he also served Bradford City. In January 1957 Galbraith had signed Anders from Avenue for Accrington Stanley.

Unbeaten York City came to Bradford and figured in a 3-3 draw, memorable for Charlie Atkinson's individual goal - he dispossessed one opponent, beat two more and put it away.

Next up, Northampton - and Avenue's first home defeat for a year. This was followed by failure at York - but Bert Gebbie, formerly of Queen of the South, made a highly impressive debut in goal.

Avenue resumed their promotion push from mid-table by defeating Exeter 5-2, though the visitors faded only after an injury had cost them their captain and diligent right-half, Arnold Mitchell.

At Gillingham, John Allan missed a first-half penalty but big inside-left Felix Reilly then claimed a hat-trick.

The home fixture against Barrow was Joe Hooley's match. In for the injured Gibson, he scored twice and made two more for Allan. Right-back Gerry Lightowler "played with coolness and intelligence."

Bradford were now fifth and stayed in that area to the end of the year. They had the elasticity of Gebbie in goal, the midfield work-rate and inspiration of Charlie Atkinson, the tactical flair of Wattie Dick, the goal poaching of Allan, the craft and goal sense of Jock Buchanan and the possibility of a brilliant show on either wing from Gibson or Anders.

Supporters were shocked in January, however, when manager Galbraith left to take over at Tranmere. He had turned down their initial approach but when they renewed their bid he changed his mind. Chairman Wilson Hirst and the board then made one of the best-ever directorial moves by bringing Newcastle United and Scottish international right-half Jimmy Scoular to Avenue as player-manager

Stocky, tough, thighs thick as an oak, Scoular had been outstanding in the 1955 cup final when his "bishop's move" of long diagonal passes to the elegant Bobby Mitchell at outside-left had undone Manchester City. Now he brought that same style with him and opened out Avenue's cultured play which sometimes became clogged by muddy wintry pitches.

His capture certainly caught the imagination of Bradford enthusiasts and his debut put an extra 5,000 on the gate. It was against Aldershot and a Buchanan goal gave Bradford both points. They actually collected 12 of the 16 available in Scoular's first eight appearances as his generalship, strength and experience quickly stamped a vivid imprint on the club's promotion chances.

Atkinson, reliable anywhere on the field, moved into the forward line and was joined on February 24 by Scoular's first signing, 19-year-old Tommy Spratt, an inside-forward schooled by Manchester United who had caps at schoolboy and youth level. Allan was the man to give way to a young raider of percipience and snap shooting who hit the only goal on his debut at home to Southport on February 25.

Bert Gebbie played a blinder in a goalless draw at Darlington which was the fifth match out of seven in which he kept a clean sheet. Don McCalman commanded the middle and everyone around him hit form together in one of the season's best results when Bradford beat leaders Crystal Palace 3-1 in the following match which lifted them to third.

The next "biggie" - second-placed Peterborough at home - had to be postponed because of snow. By the time Posh came they were clear leaders but again Avenue delighted their fans - 20,461 were there to roar them on - by winning with a goal from Felix Reilly after Spratt had missed a penalty. And they were without Scoular who was sidelined with flu.

When Bradford defeated Millwall 2-1 on April 24 it was their fifth successive victory by the odd goal in 13 days and it clinched promotion from the Fourth Division (now called League Two).

PROFESSIONAL PLAYERS 1960-61

Name	Birthplace	Previous Club	Height	Weight
Goalkeepers				
H Hough	Sheffield	Barnsley	5-11	12-5
RW Routledge	Ashington	Sunderland	5-8½	10-12
A Alexander	Cumbernauld	Glenluce A.	5-11	10-1
RBR Gebbie	Cambuslang	Queen of the South	5-8½	10-2
Full Backs				
G Lightowler	Bradford	St Bede's OB	5-7½	10-10
G Baker	South Hiendley		6-0½	13-2
J Walker	Aberdeen	Aberdeen	5-10½	12-8
J Baillie	Glasgow	Leicester City	5-10	12-0
HM Lawton	Leeds	Leeds Utd	5-8½	11-2
Half Backs				
C Atkinson	Hull	Hull City.	5-8½	12-2
J Ashworth	Leeds	Ashley Road M	5-11½	10-11
DS McCalman	Greenock	Hibernian	5-11½	12-1
PW Dick	Newmains	Accrington S.	5-9	11-0
P Flynn	Glasgow	Leeds Utd	5-8½	10-11
J Scoular	Livingstone	Newcastle Utd	5-7½	12-0
Forwards				
A McHard	Dumbarton	Clyde	5-9:	10-10
IS Gibson	Newton Stewart	Accrington S.	5-5½	10-0
J Brownlee	Glasgow	Clyde	5-9	11-0
J McAllister	Barrhead	Morton	5-9	11-0
J Allan	Stirling	Third Lanark	5-8½	11-7
J Buchanan	Castlecary	Derby County	5-9	12-3
TW Dick	Glasgow	Third Lanark	5-8½	10-5
JW Hooley	Hoyland	Holbeach U	5-8½	11-10
F Reilly	Annathill	Portsmouth	5-9½	12-7
R Byrom	Blackburn	Accrington S.	5-5½	10-2
J Anders	St Helens	Buxton	5-5½	10-7
T Spratt	Cambois, nr Blyth	Man. Utd	5-8	10-4

Division Four, 1960-61

	p	w	d	l	f	a	pts	Home: w	d	l	f	a	Away: w	d	l	f	a
Peterborough Utd.	46	28	10	8	134	65	66	18	3	2	85	30	10	7	6	49	35
Crystal Palace	46	29	6	11	110	69	64	16	4	3	64	28	13	2	8	46	41
Northampton Town	46	25	10	11	90	62	60	16	4	3	53	25	9	6	8	37	37
Bradford Park Ave.	46	26	8	12	84	74	60	16	5	2	49	22	10	3	10	35	52
York City	46	21	9	16	80	60	51	17	3	3	50	14	4	6	13	30	46
Millwall	46	21	8	17	97	86	50	13	3	7	56	33	8	5	10	41	53
Darlington	46	18	13	15	78	70	49	11	7	5	41	24	7	6	10	37	46
Workington	46	21	7	18	74	76	49	14	3	6	38	28	7	4	12	36	48
Crewe Alexandra	46	20	9	17	61	67	49	11	4	8	40	29	9	5	9	21	38
Aldershot	46	18	9	19	79	69	45	16	4	3	55	19	2	5	16	24	50
Doncaster Rovers	46	19	7	20	76	78	45	15	0	8	52	33	4	7	12	24	45
Oldham Athletic	46	19	7	20	79	88	45	13	4	6	57	38	6	3	14	22	50
Stockport County	46	18	9	19	57	66	45	14	4	5	31	21	4	5	14	26	45
Southport	46	19	6	21	69	67	44	12	6	5	47	27	7	0	16	22	40
Gillingham	46	15	13	18	64	66	43	9	7	7	45	34	6	6	11	19	32
Wrexham	46	17	8	21	62	56	42	12	4	7	38	22	5	4	14	24	34
Rochdale	46	17	8	21	60	66	42	13	7	3	43	19	4	1	18	17	47
Accrington Stanley	46	16	8	22	74	88	40	12	4	7	44	32	4	4	15	30	56
Carlisle United	46	13	13	20	61	79	39	10	7	6	43	37	3	6	14	18	42
Mansfield Town	46	16	6	24	71	78	38	10	3	10	39	34	6	3	14	32	44
Exeter City	46	14	10	22	66	94	38	12	3	8	39	32	2	7	14	27	62
Barrow	46	13	11	22	52	79	37	10	6	7	33	28	3	5	15	19	51
Hartlepools United	46	12	8	26	71	103	32	10	4	9	46	40	2	4	17	25	63
Chester	46	11	9	26	61	104	31	9	7	7	38	35	2	2	19	23	69

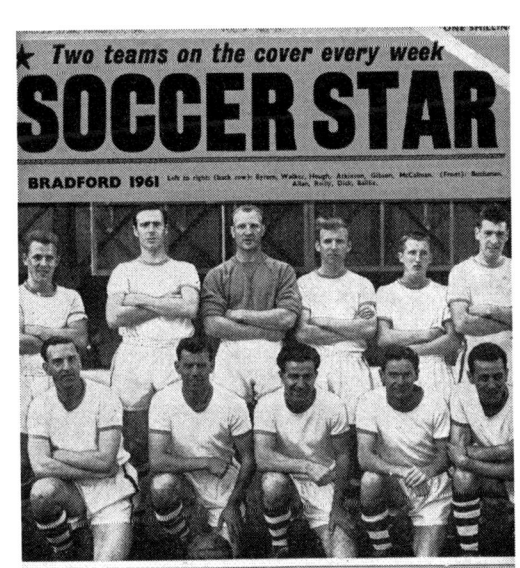

The weekly Soccer Star magazine of February 25, 1961, associate editor Jack Rollin, with Avenue on the cover. Back row: Byrom, Walker, Hough, Atkinson, Gibson, McCalman. Front: Buchanan, Allan, Reilly, Dick, Baillie

WHEN AVENUE STOOD ALONGSIDE CHELSEA

To appreciate the full flavour of Avenue's fruitful days of 1964 - the last time it was a real pleasure to watch them - it is necessary to start at the first day of spring.

On March 21, 1964, Avenue lost 2-1 at Halifax and had only three teams beneath them in Division Four. For the next match at Workington Sam Lawrie came in at outside-right and the side struck promotion form on the run-in, six victories and three draws elevating them to a finishing rung of 13th.

When the new season opened, then, not only did they begin with an unbeaten run of nine matches but they were also defending a home record which showed they had not been mastered at Park Avenue since December 28, 1963 (when Lincoln scored the only goal).

Bradford began 1964-5 with a bang. Inside 15 minutes they were three up on Doncaster at Avenue as they laid on the sort of entertainment their fans could appreciate. On the right Lawrie and Hector were in irresistible mood with Jim Fryatt the danger man in the middle. Hector notched three and made others for Lawrie and Fryatt. In defence it was Geoff Thomas who took the eye with an immaculate full-back display.

At Aldershot play became over-physical after Kearns had given the home side an early headed lead. Hector was again impressive and it was when he was brought down late on that Ronnie Bird took the chance to equalise from the spot. In the second half John Hardie brought off several brilliant saves while Bird produced the best shot from open play which home goalie David Jones turned round the post.

"The goal-getting genius of Kevin Hector, Bradford's young inside-right, already promises to become a statistical phenomenon," forecast Dick Williamson after he scored his second hat-trick of the campaign in the third match at Chesterfield. His first came in 13 minutes; then Hunt (17m) and Watkins (47m) put the Spireites in front. They were good value for their lead and were dominating play when half-way through the second half Bradford hit a rich purple passage with Fryatt and Hector (2) tearing the match wide open with three in six minutes. Hector "demonstrated hair-trigger reflexes which bode ill for Fourth Division defences this season."

On August 31 Aldershot travelled up to Avenue and surprised the crowd by their fine play. Then goalie Jones broke a leg in the 19th minute and after that it was a rearguard defence for the Soldiers who fought a good fight with all their might but surrendered goals to Fryatt, McCalman and a Bird penalty.

(We don't count Avenue's next outing because it was in the League Cup which Doncaster won by the only goal and it was reported that Hector was paying the penalty for his prolific scoring - "he will be guarded as tightly as one of the great train robbery bandits.")

Back to league matters against Notts County Bird scored his third penalty in four league matches in a 2-2 home draw.

Avenue went top - and in what better way than in wining 2-0 at Valley Parade? Jim Fryatt saw a header hooked off the line by Bruce Stowell in the first half while at the other end Peter Wragg let fly from 30 yards, John Hardie touched the ball on to the bar and caught it as it came down while he was sitting on the ground! After half-time Lawrie made a goal for Hector and then centred for Geoff Gould to head in. Gould - "a joy to watch at times" - was making his first appearance of the season after nine games in the previous two campaigns and not for the only time Don McCalman blocked the middle of the defence.

When Halifax were sent home on the wrong end of a 3-2 score-line it was the first time Bradford had ever avoided defeat in a season's opening seven matches. Town never contained the ubiquitous Hector and were also confused by some shrewd play by Fryatt. Outside-left Fidler was a Halifax danger and he scored one, made another and was near to snatching what would have been a fortunate point but the attack was foiled by John Hardie.

Another derby match - THE derby - followed when City came across from Valley Parade and took part in a storming match which sent 13,106 home with plenty to enthuse over. Peter Flynn put Avenue ahead but Steve Ingle, youngest player on the pitch at 17, startled everyone by the nature of a 30-yard drive to equalise. After 59 minutes Mike Hellawell put City in front after Hardie had kept out a power drive from John Hall. Just past the hour Jones notched the second long-distance goal of this thriller. Four minutes left and the crowd were in uproar as each side battled for full points. Then that man Hector seemed to have given Avenue the spoils - only for Price to level in the last minute after a defensive slip-up.

Another home draw followed, with Newport County. There was a lovely opener by Hector but in the end Lawrie's goal with only two minutes left was needed to preserve immunity from defeat. Much was owed to McCalman again, even though Avenue had more of the play.

They were Division Four leaders and one of only two teams unbeaten in nine Football League fixtures. The other club were Chelsea, top of the First Division.

Travelling supporters were furious when Flynn seemed to be fouled without the Crewe perpetrator being penalised as Alexandra swept on to take the lead on September 26. Hector levelled and Hunter apparently gave Bradford the lead, the referee awarding the goal, but then he consulted a linesman and changed his mind.

A fourth home draw in a row argued a strain on confidence and composure as Wrexham's strong - in all ways - defence kept Bradford at bay. Avenue had the better of the exchanges but Fryatt had one of those days when his flair for finishing deserted him

Bradford recovered their touch when Darlington were their guests, Gould giving them a warmly acclaimed opening goal. Darlo's Jimmy Lawton levelled but Fryatt cooked up two in the last quarter-hour.

The 13th league match of the season proved the unlucky one. Wrexham were too strong and although the 4-1 result flattered the Welsh club in an entertaining match, Avenue's marvellous run at last hit the buffers.

Their unbeaten home record, however, was maintained for a long time after that and was not brought to an end until February 6 when despite a brace from Fryatt, Crewe Alexandra triumphed 3-2.

Team: John Hardie; Gerry Lightowler, Ken Jones; Mal Cook, Don McCalman, Peter Flynn; Sam Lawrie, Kevin Hector Jim Fryatt, Willie Hunter, Ronnie Bird/Geoff Gould.

END OF THE ROAD

After Bradford lost their Football League place in 1970 the directors voted to carry on and an application was made for membership of the Northern Premier League. At the League's A.G.M. in Leeds, Bradford were one of six clubs elected for the 1970-1 season.

The team recovered well after a shaky start, but when chairman Herbert Metcalfe died suddenly in October 1970 the club's future was put in doubt once again. The Stockport-based businessman had been ploughing money into the club for some time and the directors were forced to reduce the wage bill. As a result many of the players who had been with the club in the Football League moved on and less experienced ones brought in struggled to make an impression.

As the team slipped down the league manager Frank Tomlinson departed and was replaced by Tony Leighton, a former favourite at Huddersfield Town and Bradford City.

It took Avenue many months to adjust to life as a non-league outfit and this was reflected in the results. The team finished 14th in 1971 and four places lower in 1972.

A Board meeting in 1968. Left to right: G Brigg (secretary), G Hudson (Supporters' Club), S Pearson (Telegraph & Argus), R Ambler (Chairman), D McCalman (manager), G Sutcliffe and M Brown (directors)

But Leighton worked hard to turn things round and the club enjoyed some long overdue success in 1972-3 following the arrival of Frank Beaumont, Mick Walker, Norman Corner and Mick Fleming, who all added some much-needed experience to the team. That season proved to be the last at Park Avenue.

In order to settle mounting debts the directors were forced to sell the Park Avenue ground which was eventually bought without planning permission by a Leeds-based property company. The local council had offered the club £80,000, which had been described as 'derisory' by club chairman George Sutcliffe. The property company acquired the ground for a sum in excess of that offered by the council, but not over £100,000.

The last league match at Park Avenue was played on April 21 1973, when Great Harwood were defeated by 2-1 before a crowd of 1,413. The points ensured Avenue finished in 5th place. A ground-sharing agreement was reached with neighbours Bradford City for the 1973-4 season, but this did not prove a success.

With continuing financial problems (the club had received an unexpected Capital Gains Tax bill for the sale of Park Avenue), dwindling support and poor results the directors decided to close the club down at the end of the season. Roy Ambler had taken over the reigns as team boss when Leighton and the club parted company in November and results had improved, but there was to be no last-minute reprieve.

Avenue did manage to finish on a winning note beating Great Harwood with a Fleming goal watched by a Valley Parade crowd of just 698.

The club was officially wound up at a creditors' meeting at the Midland Hotel in Bradford on May 3. A tax bill of £7,777 formed the majority of the deficiency of £9,386.

June 1970: Mike Walker, Alan Roberts, Harry Preece and Tony Woolmer discuss their futures following the club's expulsion from the Football League.

PHOENIX

In 1975, a year after the demise of the Park Avenue club, a small band of supporters formed a local Sunday side in order to keep the name alive. Their aim was to return to Saturday soccer on a semi-professional basis, but as the years went by it became clear that this was not going to happen. In fact 12 years passed before a serious revival bid got underway; this came in the form of a campaign launched in the city during 1987 by Bob Robinson and supported by former Avenue star Kevin Hector. Robinson's ambitious plans included resurrecting the Bradford club and restoring it back in the Football League. It was soon made known that any new club would not be able to use the football ground at Park Avenue as part of it had been earmarked for redevelopment. In the meantime representatives of the Sunday side agreed to join forces with Robinson and it was all systems go. It had been agreed that the Sunday team could continue. In June 1988 it was announced that the new club had been accepted by the West Riding County Amateur League.

Bob Robinson

After the re-formation, a side capable of holding its own in the County Amateur League was put together at short notice by Bob Wood. The team had a mixed start after beating Salts 3-2 at Manningham Mills in the opening match watched by an expectant crowd of 350, and it wasn't long before Wood stood aside to allow the committee to appoint Mick Hall as player-manager. Hall, who had had plenty of experience in the County Amateur League, brought several players from his old club Birkenshaw Rovers and the team settled near the top of the Third Division. However, they never quite made up for their indifferent start and finished runners-up. The Avenue committee looked towards the Northern Counties East League as they sought advancement, but were met with a rebuttal. Instead, chairman Robinson had discussions with an old contact, Frank Harwood of the Central Midlands League. Harwood convinced the CML to fast-track Avenue, Hucknall Town and Long Eaton United into the Supreme Division and nearly split the League in doing so, but Avenue were given the nod provided that they found a suitable stadium. There being none available in Bradford, Bramley's McLaren Field was hired and the club moved into exile.

1989: Mick Hall in determined mood in a friendly with Bradford City

With a much tougher campaign ahead, Hall assembled almost an entire new team, drafting in players from the

38

Premier Division of the County Amateur League. Many of these went on to give lengthy service to Avenue and included Billy Payton, Peter Edmondson and Darren Wardman who clocked up over 500 appearances between them. The League programme set off in fine style, but sadly it was a false dawn; form declined and attendances plummeted. After a 6-0 drubbing at Gainsborough Town, Hall was asked to resign. The board quickly appointed former Avenue full-back Jim Mackay, who had been successful as manager with Thackley and Pontefract Collieries. Mackay immediately brought in Rohan Eli, Andy Watmuff and Bob Mackay to bolster the squad and by the New Year the side was further strengthened by the addition of Doug Saunders and Paul Allen. But Avenue struggled to make home advantage count and in losing half of their 38 matches finished fifth from bottom. In December, though, Avenue's board had mixed good fortune with prescience, resigning from the CML when it became clear that the League would not be achieving its desired place on the pyramid. In order to protect the League the FA slapped an embargo on other clubs defecting so only Avenue and Ilkeston could escape.

Avenue were successful with their application to join the North West Counties League in the summer of 1990. This gave the club a foothold on the pyramid and the opportunity to regain their place in the Football League. The squad was further strengthened for the difficult challenge ahead, Mackay signing Andy Pickles, Rupert Eli, Carl Slater and Craig Sidda. The team maintained a challenging position throughout the season, but it was in the West Riding County Cup where they excelled, despatching Hatfield Main 5-1 and then formidable Goole Town 3-0 before facing Farsley Celtic in the quarter finals at Throstle Nest. In a rain-lashed game Avenue pulled off another shock beating their local rivals 2-1 to earn a semi-final date at Garforth Town. Another fine away victory saw Avenue book a place in the final at Valley Parade against Pontefract Collieries. And before a four-figure crowd Mackay's battlers lifted the cup thanks to a late burst of goals after Edmondson had grabbed an equaliser on 85 minutes to take the match into extra-time.

In the League Avenue couldn't overhaul Blackpool Rovers in second spot but heard on the quiet that the league planned to promote the third-placed team to equalise the divisions. This should have been a formality but Salford City, who faced relegation from the top division, persuaded the AGM to vote it out. Avenue were marooned; however Glossop North End canvassed enough support to hold an EGM and Avenue were up.

The team made a promising start to the 1991-2 campaign, and things were looking good into the New Year with Peter Craven slotting in well in his first spell with the club and Wardman continuing to bang in the goals. But the players suddenly lost confidence and following a disastrous run of results the team dropped from sixth to just above the relegation zone. Meanwhile hopes of another County Cup Final appearance had disappeared with a 5-2 semi-final defeat at Goole.

When Avenue completed their league programme with a home defeat to Atherton LR, the teams around them still had games to play. And they all climbed above Avenue except Bootle, who were also experiencing some dire results. The Merseysiders needed to win their final game to survive but could only manage a 1-1 draw and Avenue held on to their First Division place by the skin of their teeth.

With Wardman making himself unavailable, Avenue supporters were expecting another hard struggle in 1992-3 but the defence had been stiffened by the arrival of goalkeeper Gary Cox along with Tony Pearson and Graham Jones. The results of this were immediately apparent as the miserly defence took Avenue to a comfortable league place. The team also enjoyed an historic FA Cup qualifying appearance at Accrington Stanley where the UniBond outfit claimed a 2-0 victory.

Sep 12 1992: Andy Watmuff in action against Belper Town in the FA Cup

Sep 26 1992: Cup tie at Accrington Stanley. (Below) Tony Pearson is about to tackle an Accrington player, and (right) Rohan Eli in action.

One blot on the landscape was the continuing deterioration of McLaren Field. Avenue's first home match had to be postponed when Bramley boss Maurice Bamford didn't allow the grass to be cut! The floodlights were unreliable and the general state of disrepair was such that the NWCL insisted on action. A chance encounter between Alan Sutcliffe and Batley RLFC chairman Steve Ball led to Avenue moving on to Kirklees, even further away from Bradford.

The summer of 1993 saw the club settling in at Mount Pleasant, but Mackay soon had to contend with an injury to Rohan Eli who had been outstanding the previous season. Without adequate replacements the team struggled resulting in the departure of Mackay who decided to resign following a humbling 6-0 defeat to Skelmersdale United. The Avenue board turned to Gordon Rayner and Dave Heeley who had been sensationally sacked by Guiseley at the end of the previous campaign. Their new club, Glossop North End, agreed to release the pair and Rayner quickly turned over most of the playing staff. However, despite signings like Mark Wilson, Lee Williams, Paul Laycock and Paul Viner, Avenue flirted with relegation until everything came right in March and they stormed up to an unlikely mid-table finish.

With Lee Margerison, Mark Price and Dave Morgan recruited, Rayner's first full season in charge got away to a flying start and the team soon surged to the top of the division. They also threatened to do well in the FA Vase, but after seeing off South Normanton Athletic, when at one stage they were 0-3 down, and St Helens Town, a poor performance against Eastwood Hanley, when Wilson was dismissed, brought the run to a disappointing end. Wilson was soon on his way to Emley with Paul Viner and Matt Johnson coming in the opposite direction.

Avenue's league form took an unexpected turn just after Christmas and by the time promotion rivals Clitheroe beat them in March the Lancastrians were 20 points ahead and seemingly had the title in the bag. Rayner had to act swiftly. He bolstered his squad by bringing in strikers Darron Morris and Tony Marshall and suddenly the team was transformed and embarked on a winning run. With Clitheroe and St Helens dropping vital points, Avenue gradually cut the gap between themselves and the leaders and a record 13 consecutive wins proved enough to clinch the championship, two goals from Morris against Bacup Borough doing the trick at Mount Pleasant. The club was then rocked when the UniBond League announced that runners-up Clitheroe would be promoted since Avenue's ground at Horsfall Stadium was not ready. Avenue protested that Mount Pleasant was still their home and thankfully the FA appeal committee agreed.

Gordon Rayner

1995-6 proved to be Avenue's final season sharing with Batley with a move back to Bradford expected in the summer of 1996. After a spluttering start the team eventually found their feet in the UniBond First Division, but good results at home were hard to come by. Among several new signings was Chris Brandon who was to go on and carve out a career in the Football League. Rayner, though, relied on much of the squad which had won the NWCL championship and it was clear that a mid-table finish was the best that could be hoped for in a strong division. Supporters were able to enjoy a long FA Cup run which took the club to the brink of the first round proper. A satisfying victory at Accrington was the highlight before Marine ended hopes of a big pay-day by claiming a 2-0 fourth qualifying round victory on Merseyside. Avenue only managed three wins at Mount Pleasant but six on travel ensured they always had enough points on the board and relegation was never a threat. The last two games epitomised the team's form over the season: 2-0 up and dominant for over an hour only to fall to defeat in the latter stages.

After a series of poor results in the last few months of the 1995-6 season, Rayner made sweeping changes to his squad ahead of the club's eagerly awaited return to Bradford. But when the first three league matches were lost the board took action and Rayner was given the sack. By the end of September former Tranmere, Liverpool and Chester defender Trevor Storton had been installed in the hot-seat. With only a handful of changes he turned things round and the team finished 7th. Storton also guided Avenue to the second round of the FA Trophy where they were narrowly beaten by Morecambe in front of a bumper Horsfall crowd.

Performances continued to improve over the next three seasons as the club became well established in the UniBond League. Goalkeeper Paddy Kenny, who later achieved international honours while with Sheffield United, was discovered by Storton playing in the County Amateur League and brought to Avenue in 1997. Another of Storton's shrewd signings was striker Jason Maxwell who went on to give long and loyal service to the club. Also on board were Clive Freeman and Phil Sharpe (later to form the club's management team) and Wayne Benn who was to become a club legend making over 400 appearances. The club enjoyed another run in the FA Trophy in 1998-9, reaching the fourth round before going out to Colwyn Bay.

Storton brought in Gavin Kelly, Mark Hancock, Martin James, Phil Denny and Martin Pemberton as he attempted another assault on the title in 1999-2000. Maxwell, Denny and Pemberton notched 43 goals between them as Avenue claimed 4th place. But it all came together in 2000-1 with Ian Thompson now assistant manager. Storton's master-stroke was the signing of striker Andy Hayward from Frickley for a reported £2,000 fee. The former Barrow marksman hit 22 league goals with Maxwell chipping in with a further 18 as Avenue won the championship by ten clear points. The title was won on the back of an excellent late run which saw the team win 14 of their final 18 games.

Storton kept faith with his championship-winning squad for the 2001-2 season, but when the team failed to win any of their opening twelve games relegation fears arose. However, a 3-0 success against Frickley on October 2 sparked a recovery and six wins from their last seven outings catapulted them to a top ten finish. That season Avenue reached the League Cup final only to lose out to

July 1994, a pre-season friendly with Bradford City; Messrs Morgan, Taylor, Goddard and Forrest keep an eye on the action.

42

Accrington following a penalty shoot-out. Two larger-than-life characters to emerge during 2002-3 were flying winger Rory Prendergast and Lutz Pfannenstiel, a German-born goalkeeper. Prendergast terrorised defences with his electrifying pace and spectacular goals and it was no surprise when Accrington obtained his signature just before Christmas. Pfannenstiel, a bit of an oddball, soon endeared himself to supporters, but he almost lost his life on Boxing Day after a collision with a Harrogate Town player. Luckily, Avenue physio Ray Killick saved the day when he gave the unconscious goalkeeper mouth-to-mouth resuscitation after he stopped breathing three times. Storton guided Avenue into seventh spot and their highest placing in the UniBond League during his stewardship. Despite the arrival of the experienced Carl Serrant, Ryan Crossley and Steve Oleksewycz, Avenue struggled in their third season in the top tier, but some poor league results were forgotten for a time as the team battled through to the FA Cup first round proper and a home clash with Bristol City. A record Horsfall crowd of 2,045 saw Avenue go out by 5-2 with heads held high.

Storton and the club parted company in March 2004 with the team hovering near the foot of the division. It was ironic that he should have reserved his poorest league campaign for 2003-4 when only a top 13 finish was needed to book a place in the newly-created Conference North. But all was not lost. The board quickly appointed former Sheffield Wednesday, Leeds United and Bradford City star Carl Shutt as manager and in the ten remaining games the team collected 16 points to secure a place in the play-offs for the right to take the fourteenth 'promotion' berth. And a fairytale ending was assured when Avenue knocked out Burscough by 2-0 in the final after getting past Spennymoor and Ashton United.

Money was in short supply for Shutt to strengthen the team for what would clearly be an uphill struggle in Conference North: with the likes of Kettering Town, Stafford Rangers, Worcester City and Southport to play Avenue were now a little fish in a big pool. There was no way they could match most of their rivals' spending power. But to be fair the team performed to the best of their ability, but it wasn't enough and with only two wins from 16 games they soon became one of the favourites to make the drop. In a desperate attempt to turns things round Shutt put himself on the team sheet but it was all to no avail. Supporters became

Steve Oleksewycz fires home Avenue's opener in the 2-0 play-off victory against Burscough, May 2004

disillusioned and attendances dropped; and the team's fate was sealed long before the end of April. A miserable season closed with Avenue bottom of the table with just 24 points. Not surprisingly Shutt left Horsfall during the summer and his replacement was ex-Ossett Town boss Gary Brook.

Back in the UniBond Premier and there were mixed views on how the team would perform. Many pundits had Avenue making a swift return to the Conference, but there were several long-standing supporters who predicted another struggle against relegation. Brook used his contacts to overhaul the squad, and it appeared he had found a winning formula when the team reached the top four at the end of October. The excellent start had included a stunning 6-3 win at title favourites AFC Telford. But it all went awry after that. From November onwards the team started to slide down the division and in collecting just 11 points from 26 games they suffered a second successive relegation. The board left it rather late to hand Brook his cards and when Phil Sharpe and assistant Clive Freeman took over the former Avenue favourites found the ship sinking faster than the Titanic; despite a few encouraging results they were forced to accept the inevitable.

In 2006-7 Avenue's success-starved supporters looked to Sharpe and Freeman to right the ship and this they did. The duo turned to former Avenue team-mates to form the backbone of the squad with Mark Wilson, Stephen Ball, Lee Connor and Scott Jackson enjoying another stint at Horsfall. The team's success was built on a mean defence with Gary Shaw an outstanding figure and Avenue were always in the hunt for a play-off spot after Buxton set the pace and could not be caught. Avenue was 41-year-old Neil Redfearn's port of call during 2006-7. The former Premiership star agreed to be part of manager Phil Sharpe's squad on a non-contract basis in the summer after leaving Scarborough where he had been manager for just over six months. Redfearn had a strong link to Park Avenue as his father, Brian, turned out for the club during the 1950s. After appearing on 790 occasions in the Football League the Dewsbury-born midfielder currently stands fifth in the list of most appearances behind such luminaries as Peter Shilton (1,005), Tony Ford (938), Terry Paine (824) and Tommy Hutchison (794). Redfearn made his 1,000th career appearance in Avenue's colours when the club met Solihull Borough in the FA Trophy. Earlier in the season he scored his 200th career goal in Avenue's 7-3 league defeat of Clitheroe. A surprise moved to UniBond rivals Stocksbridge Park Steels before the end of the season ended his brief spell with the club.

Avenue hit the headlines in March 2007 when local businessman Robert Blackburn became the club's new owner after acquiring the shareholding of former chairman Frank Thornton. Blackburn went on record to say he intended to get Park Avenue back in the Football League within five years. Sharpe and Freeman agreed to stand aside when Blackburn persuaded Witton Albion assistant boss Benny Phillips to take over the reins in a full-time capacity. Money was quickly made available for the squad to be increased ahead of the transfer deadline. The new recruits, including former Bradford City striker Kevin Sanasy and Stalybridge's Dominic Krief, looked to have given the side the strength to win promotion through the play-offs. They fought off their rivals for a play-off place and in finishing fourth had to visit third-placed Eastwood Town. But it all ended in tears. A big Avenue following at Coronation Park could only watch in disbelief as their favourites failed to rise to the occasion. Eastwood then underlined their promotion credentials knocking out runners-up Cammell Laird in the final to join Buxton in the Premier Division. For Avenue it remained a case of what might have been; however supporters could at least look forward to a new season as the Blackburn revolution gathered pace.

PARK AVENUE MONTH BY MONTH

JANUARY

Bradford beat Workington at Park Avenue in an FA Cup tie in January 1936, with Sam Doran scoring the winning goal two minutes from time. The match receipts (£639) and attendance (10,706) were the lowest on the day in the third round.

The first all-ticket match in Bradford football history attracted a crowd of 24,270 in January 1947, to watch Manchester United at Park Avenue in the FA Cup third round. The club actually sold 26,900 tickets bringing in receipts of £2,935.

Player-manager Jimmy Scoular was suspended for 28 days in January 1964 and fined 20 guineas after being sent off in a home game against Gillingham.

In January 1913, Second Division Bradford beat non-league Barrow at Park Avenue by 1-0 in an FA Cup replay after the Lancashire outfit had been paid £650 to waive ground rights. Snow had caused a postponement on the original date and the teams had then played a 1 - 1 draw at Park Avenue.

Stanley Matthews made his first appearance in Bradford as Stoke City's outside-right in a drawn fourth round FA Cup-tie at Park Avenue during January 1938.

Bradford's appearance at Plymouth Argyle for an FA Cup-tie in January 1929 set a new ground record attendance of 33,050.

The first case of a Bradford player being chosen for an international match while attached to the club was that of Sam Burnison in January 1911, who was the Ireland right-back against Wales at Belfast.

George Henson recorded the club's individual scoring record when he netted six times in a 7-1 home Second Division victory against Blackburn Rovers during January 1938. His goals arrived after 5, 29, 66, 78, 83 and 86 minutes. Billy Martin scored the seventh in the final minutes.

George Henson

Bradford played more locals than in any other peace-time league match in the club's history, six Bradford natives - Jeff Suddards, Dick Conroy, Dennis Brickley, Bill Deplidge, Reg Worsman and Brian Redfearn - being in the team against Crewe Alexandra at Park Avenue in January 1955.

During January 1931, Sydney Dickinson, playing at outside-left, scored three goals against Burnley at Park Avenue, two direct from corners. Bradford's other extreme winger, Bert Davis, had scored three at Southampton seven days earlier.

FEBRUARY

During February 1928, Ken McDonald scored his 11th and last hat-trick for Bradford in a match against Tranmere Rovers - a club record.

Bradford, whose last game had been against Halifax Town on January 4 1963, ended their longest-ever run without a match due to adverse weather conditions with an away fixture at Bristol City on February 16.

Tommy Tomlinson hit a home hat-trick on his Football League debut against Grimsby Town in February 1910 to create a club record. And after leading by 1-0 at half-time, Bradford netted five more after the break to end up 6-1 winners.

During 1935-6, Bradford finally overcame FA Cup fourth round opponents West Bromwich Albion by 2-0 in a second replay staged at Old Trafford. It was estimated that 1,230 supporters made the journey to Manchester by train.

When Bradford signed Brentford's inside-right George Wilkins for £6,500 in February 1947 they broke the club record for a fee paid for the third time in a month. During January the record had been broken twice on the same day when an undisclosed fee secured Bill Woods from Rochdale and a few hours later £6,000 was paid to Reading for Bill Layton.

A blinding snowstorm caused Bradford's First Division meeting with Everton to be abandoned after 35 minutes in February 1915, several visiting players having complained of exhaustion after facing the blizzard. The abnormal conditions had helped Bradford into a 3-0 lead; however Everton won the replayed match by 2-1.

Bradford's first-ever Sunday engagement was against Hyde United in the North West Floodlit League at Park Avenue in February 1972.

On February 21, 1914, Bradford won an away match by 6-1 at Fulham after the home side had scored first. It was the club's first victory in London in the Second Division after their previous 14 visits had all ended in defeat.

The first annual trip of the Bradford club as an association organisation took place during February 1908 when the team travelled to meet Queens Park Rangers in the Southern League.

During February 1937 Bradford surrendered a match-winning 3-0 interval lead to lose their Second Division home game by 5-4 to Chesterfield.

MARCH

From 1911 until 1924 Bradford played under manager Tom Maley in a green and white strip. But on March 1, 1924, just a few days after he resigned, the club returned to their former red, amber and black colours in a home Third Division (North) match against Crewe.

When inside forward Johnny Downie left for Old Trafford as a replacement for the departed Johnny Morris in March 1949, Bradford received £20,000 which was a record fee paid to any West Riding club.

Former international goalkeeper Tom Baddeley, who had been on holiday, caused problems for manager Fred Halliday when he missed his train at Birmingham in March 1908. As a result Halliday was forced to deputise between the posts in a Southern League defeat at Swindon.

Johnny Downie

During a Third Division (North) match at Crewe on March 8, 1924, Bradford conceded four penalties but still managed to return home with a point in a 1-1 draw. Goalkeeper Alf Laycock deputising for regular custodian Ernald Scattergood, saved the first spot-kick and then saw the second go wide. The third was sent against the crossbar by Goodwin and Doran, who had failed with the first two, converted the fourth.

Bradford's Second Division game at Notts County on March 10, 1934, began in spring-like weather only to be held up after 10 minutes due to a violent storm and torrential rainfall. After a halt of 10 minutes the game was restarted, but after it had gone on for seven more minutes it was abandoned because the playing area was under water.

March 12, 1947, and Bradford's midweek Second Division meeting with Sheffield Wednesday was their first game for five and a half weeks and their first at home for seven and a half weeks - both were club records. Their League games on five consecutive Saturdays had all been postponed - the first because Wednesday were engaged in the FA Cup and the other four through snow and ice.

When Leon Leuty moved to Park Avenue from Derby County in March 1950 the fee paid by Bradford of £24,500 was the second largest in Football League history (the record was held by Preston for the transfer of inside forward Eddie Quigley from Sheffield Wednesday in 1949) and £8,000 more than the previous highest paid by any club for a centre-half.

A Third Division (North) match between Bradford and Barrow on the afternoon of Wednesday March 17, 1954, attracted a record low attendance of 1,881 to Park Avenue which brought receipts of just £147.

In a home game against Durham City on March 22, 1924, Bradford played their ninth local of the season in Albert Bradley - a club record.

George Turnbull, a left-back, died in Bradford Royal Infirmary on March 25, 1928, after suffering a fractured skull when falling off a motor cycle he was riding earlier in the day. He had played for Bradford's second team the previous day in an away Midland League match at Hull City.

Bradford appointed George Brigg as secretary on March 28, 1934, which was during the same week as Billy Hardy became manager. When Bradford lost their Football League status in 1970 Brigg still held that post and was the longest-serving secretary in the League.

On March 29, 1924, Charles Parker, who had earlier accepted the position of manager following the resignation of Tom Maley, suddenly withdrew his acceptance and returned to Preston North End.

March 31, 1920, saw the untimely death of Bradford chairman Harry Briggs. The club's greatest benefactor and chairman for 20 years passed away peacefully at his home in Cottingley aged 56, leaving a personal fortune of £243,000.

On March 31, 1934, Bradford played their 12th and last Football League game against Lincoln City up to the start of the 1939-45 war, the series starting in 1909-10 season, and won every game outright with a goals record of 45-5.

APRIL

Everton's 'Dixie' Dean registered his 200th goal on April 4, 1931, during his side's 4-2 home victory against Bradford in the Second Division. The match at Goodison Park attracted 32,213, which was the highest crowd Bradford played in front of that season.

George Halley became the first Bradford player to be sent off during an away Second Division match at Bristol City on Easter Monday, 1912.

On April 8, 1926, George McLean began a suspension which ran until the end of the season and continued over the first few weeks of the following campaign until September 30. The ban was the result of misconduct in a reserve match at Halifax on March 30.

Ace marksman Kevin Hector's hat-trick at Chester on April 8, 1966, included his 100th Football League goal. His age at the time was 21 years and 156 days. This record had been bettered only twice before by Jimmy Greaves (20, 261) and 'Dixie' Dean (20, 324).

On April 15, 1966, Kevin Hector, in an away match against Barnsley, made his 156th consecutive Football League appearance thereby creating a new Bradford record beating the 155 match run made equally by Jack Scott (April

6, 1912 to April 6, 1920) and Don McCalman (February 27, 1960 to August 26, 1963).

Bradford's lowest-ever peacetime Saturday crowd for a Football League fixture - just 1,780 - watched the Fourth Division match against Workington on April 19, 1969.

On April 20, 1970, Bradford played their very last Football League match and lost 4-2 at Aldershot. It was the club's 56th away League game without a win.

Jim Fryatt got himself in the record books after scoring the fastest-ever Football League goal in a home match against Tranmere Rovers on April 25, 1964. His goal in a 4-2 win came after just four seconds, according to the referee.

Bradford beat Blackpool at Park Avenue on April 25, 1914, by 4-1 and won promotion to the First Division. Later at a promotion dinner at Midland Hotel, Tommy Little became the first Bradford player to receive a benefit cheque (£470).

On April 30, 1966, Kevin Hector netted twice at Crewe to break the club's scoring record set up by Ken McDonald's 43 Third Division (North) goals in season 1925-6.

MAY

Bradford's three goals at Halifax on May 2, 1925, in the final league match gave them 84 goals setting a new Northern Section record, beating Darlington's 81 in the Section's second season. Avenue subsequently raised it to 101.

On May 5, 1928, Bradford defeated New Brighton by 2-1 to win the Third Division (North) championship and completed 100 Football League goals for the third successive season.

The lowest-ever Park Avenue attendance for a Football League match - 1,572 - turned up to watch Bradford's Monday evening meeting with Port Vale on May 5, 1969.

Irvine Harwood's move from Bradford to Bradford City on May 6, 1932, became the first transfer in history between the clubs in which a fee (£250) was paid.

On May 14, 1947, 'Chick' Farr, breaking his right forearm in a home game against Manchester City, made the last of 135 consecutive Second Division appearances as Bradford's goalkeeper, the sequence having started on February 20, 1937.

Len Shackleton's first appearance with Bradford was at Park Avenue on May 20, 1940, in a match against Hartlepools United. He scored one of the goals in a 2-0 win. Alec Coxon (later Yorkshire cricketer) was Bradford's centre-forward for the first and only time in the same match.

Geoff Walker's transfer to Middlesbrough on May 23, 1946, brought Bradford a record fee of about £6,000, but this was easily beaten five months later when the club received £13,000 from Newcastle for Len Shackleton.

Bradford signed the first international in their history on May 28, 1907, when former Wolverhampton and England goalkeeper Tom Baddeley moved to Park Avenue in the build up to the club's first season in association football.

Geoff Walker

JUNE

Jack Scott, who held the club record for the most consecutive league appearances (155) was transferred to Manchester United on June 4, 1921, for a fee of £750. He had been at Park Avenue for 11 years.

June 14, 1947, and Bradford announced the purchase of the Park Avenue ground on the day the team completed the longest season in history by losing 0-4 at Nottingham Forest.

An FA commission at Sheffield on June 23, 1921, suspended David McLean from the following August 27 to November 1 and Bob Turnbull from August 27 to October 1 and prohibited Bradford from admitting boys to Park Avenue before October 1. The decisions were a sequel to events at a match against Manchester City on the previous April 30, when McLean was ordered off and stones were alleged to have been thrown at the referee.

On June 28, 1907, Bradford appointed their first trainer - Edward Kinnear, who was aged 35 and had had three years with Grimsby Town after being a Sheffield Wednesday player.

AUGUST

The first-known football match to be filmed at Park Avenue was against Derby County on August 25, 1956.

Billy Elliott was transferred to Burnley on August 31, 1951, after refusing to re-sign. The Turf Moor club paid out £20,000 for his services.

SEPTEMBER

The first competitive match in Bradford's history was in the North Eastern League on September 2, 1907. The first team was given a run out and they defeated Newcastle United reserves by 2-1 before a Park Avenue crowd of 6,000.

On September 3, 1951, Bradford paid Burnley a fee in the region of £6,000 for outside-left Terry Lyons, a local lad whom they had given two 'A' team trials three years earlier.

Bradford had 12 players in a match at Sheffield Wednesday on September 4, 1915, which they won by 4-2. Walter Cawdry kept goal for the first 25 minutes and then retired on the arrival of Ernald Scattergood.

The referee played short time at Halifax in a Third Division (North) local derby on September 5, 1925, and was forced to recall both teams for four minutes during which time the home side scored their goal in a 2-1 defeat to Bradford.

On September 6, 1952, Bradford dropped to the bottom of the Northern Section for the first time in their history with a team that was the costliest in its class.

Kevin Hector's last game for Bradford was on September 6, 1966, when he made his 166th consecutive league appearance - a club record.

The back page that told Avenue fans the news they had feared – the departure of their ace marksman marked the start of Bradford's slide out of the Football League

On September 9, 1916, Second-Lieutenant Donald Bell became the only Football League professional to be awarded the Victoria Cross in history. The former Bradford back received the medal posthumously for "most conspicuous bravery" on the Somme.

Beating Doncaster Rovers at Park Avenue on September 10, 1947, Bradford completed the best start to a season in their history in having won all their first six games.

Albert Geldard (15) and Walter Millership (19) played together as Bradford's right wing against Millwall on September 16, 1929, in a Second Division match when their combined ages were only 34 years - a Football League record at the time.

The derby between the two Bradford clubs on September 17, 1927, attracted a crowd of 38,442 to Valley Parade and was the biggest on record in the series between the wool city rivals. The match also completed the only case in history of two teams in the same provincial town or city meeting in all three Football League divisions.

On September 20, 1950, Leon Leuty was transferred to Notts County for £24,500 a few hours after David Reid had been secured from Rochdale for £5,000.

Bradford made their eighth and last Football League appearance on Clapton Orient's ground on September 22, 1928, and did not secure either a point or a goal in any of them, six being lost by 1-0 and two by 2-0.

The biggest-ever goals concession in Bradford's Football League history was in an 8-2 defeat at Port Vale in the Second Division on September 22, 1930.

A goal after just 15 seconds from Harry McIlvenny in a Second Division match at home to Cardiff City on September 24, 1949, set a new club record.

Tommy Lloyd, playing for Bradford at Park Avenue against Nottingham Forest on September 28, 1935, suffered concussion when struck on the head, but played on, and after the game he did not remember what had happened and did not know what the result was.

OCTOBER

On October 1, 1949, Bradford played before the biggest Football League crowd in their history, 54,905 seeing them lose by 5-0 to Tottenham Hotspur at White Hart Lane.

Bradford manager David Steele played at centre-forward against Sheffield Wednesday at Park Avenue in a wartime fixture on October 3, 1942, when his age exceeded by a few months the combined ages of Billy Elliott, Johnny Downie and Geoff Walker, who all figured in the team.

The first floodlit match at Park Avenue was played on October 3, 1961, when Bradford took on Czechoslovakia.

Peter O'Rourke junior, when his father was manager of the club, made a sensational Football League debut against Durham City on October 4, 1924, by scoring twice in the opening six minutes to help his team to a 4-1 victory.

The Bradford team to meet Mansfield Town at Park Avenue on October 4, 1952, included two 17-year-old forwards, Derek Kevan having been born in March, 1935, and Brian Redfearn in February, 1935. At left-back was Geoffrey Hudson, who was not 21 until the following week.

The game against Ashington on October 9, 1926, was the first of 25 consecutive home Northern Section fixtures won by Bradford - an unparalleled sequence by any team to this day in Football League history.

The programme for Bradford's first floodlit fixture

On October 10, 1925, Harold Hodgson, Bradford's left-back, broke his right leg in a collision with Tranmere centre-forward Johnson at Park Avenue, and never played again.

J W Sutcliffe was given a rapturous welcome by home supporters on October 12, 1907, when keeping goal for Plymouth Argyle in a Southern League match at Park Avenue, where he had won international rugby reputation with Bradford 20 years previously. Over 1,100 Argyle supporters made the long journey.

On October 15, 1934, a combined Bradford - Bradford City team beat a combined Huddersfield Town & Leeds United side by 3-2 at Valley Parade in a match in aid of the Gresford Colliery Disaster Fund. The game, watched by 3,193, brought in receipts of £200.

Bradford played their first League match at Park Avenue under floodlights on October 16, 1961, against Coventry City.

Bradford recorded their biggest-ever victory on October 17, 1908, when they defeated Denby Dale by 11-0 in an FA Cup qualifying round. Bradford travelled with a team made up of mainly reserve players as the first eleven had to fulfil a home Second Division fixture on the same afternoon.

On October 24, 1936, Magnus McPhee and John McCall were transferred to Bradford from Workington for about £2,000, the stipulation being made that an additional £250 would be paid if McPhee scored 20 goals in that season. He got 18.

October 24, 1942, saw the death of Fred Chadwick, who had been Bradford's trainer for 14 years covering the time the club gained promotion to the First Division in 1914. And on the same day of that month in 1970 the club was rocked by the untimely death at the age of 63 of chairman Herbert Metcalfe.

On October 28, 1910, an FA commission, on appeal, reduced from £75 to £50 a fine imposed on Bradford City by the West Riding Association for playing a weakened team against Bradford in a West Yorkshire Cup first round tie at Park Avenue during the previous month.

Bradford beat Accrington Stanley at Park Avenue by 6-4 on October 31, 1953, after leading at half-time by 1-0. The aggregate of nine goals in the second half was a record for any half of a Football League game in the club's history.

NOVEMBER

Among the 50,000 spectators at Stamford Bridge for the visit of Bradford in the First Division on November 1, 1919, was the King of Spain.

On November 1, 1910, Bradford beat Leeds City by 5-1 at Valley Parade to win the West Riding Senior Cup in the competition's first year.

A Third Division (North) fixture at Park Avenue against Halifax Town on November 5, 1927, was the last of 25 consecutive home Northern Section matches won by Bradford - an unparalleled sequence by any other Football League team in history.

The attendance for the Bradford derby at Valley Parade on November 6, 1968, was just 8,101 - the smallest-ever peacetime 'gate' in the series between the wool city rivals.

On November 8, 1952, Bradford played the first of seven consecutive home matches, the sequence comprising Crewe Alexandra, Rochdale (FA Cup), Chester, Gateshead United (FA Cup), Stockport County, York City and Halifax Town.

The official opening of the new pavilion at Park Avenue took place on November 9, 1907. Later a dinner was held at the Great Northern Victoria Hotel in the city.

On November 11, 1950, Bradford, leading by 2-1 at the interval, lost at home by 4-2 to Shrewsbury Town, who were bottom of the Northern Section. It was arguably one of the club's most humiliating defeats.

Bradford transferred Albert Geldard to Everton on November 14, 1932, when the boy prodigy was aged just 18 years and 7 months.

George McLean scored a hat-trick in his final League appearance for Bradford on November 15, 1930, against Bristol City at Park Avenue. His third and final goal gave him 136 League goals for the club and one more than Ken McDonald who had previously held the record for the most goals in aggregate.

Radio star Wilfred Pickles presented his popular show "Have A Go" from Park Avenue on November 15, 1947.

On November 16, 1907, Bradford appeared on the Cup Final ground in playing a 1-1 draw in the Southern League with Crystal Palace at Sydenham.

The first meeting in history of the Bradford clubs was on November 19, 1907, City winning a North Eastern League game at Valley Parade by 2-1. The reserve fixture attracted an attendance of 13,000 (£275).

Bradford, beaten by Doncaster Rovers on November 19, 1927, lost for the first time at home in the League since Grimsby Town lowered their colours on December 26, 1925. Between the two dates Bradford played 38 home Northern Section games, winning 34 and drawing four.

The first full-scale meeting in history of the two Bradford clubs took place on November 20, 1912, City winning by 2-0 at Valley Parade in a match for George Chaplin's benefit, and for which Mr G H Pauling presented handsome medals for the winners.

Ace marksman Kevin Hector scored five times in a 7-2 Fourth Division home victory against Barnsley on November 20, 1965. All Hector's goals came in a 27-minute spell - 30, 38, 39, 48 and 57 minutes.

Centre-forward Jimmy Smith, who was to become a crowd favourite, was transferred to Bradford for £800 from Brighton on November 22, 1912. The deal also saw Bradford inside-right Bobby Smith move to the south coast club.

Goalkeeper Tommy "Chick" Farr was married on the morning of November 23, 1935, and in the afternoon turned out for Bradford in the Second Division derby with Bradford City (1-1).

On November 26, 1949, Bradford played an all-English team for the first time since February 1, 1936, the side against Bury at Park Avenue being: Nicholls; Farrell, Hepworth; White, Horsman, Elliott; Smith, Deplidge, McIlvenny, Haines, Stevens.

An away game at Charlton Athletic on November 30, 1929, marked the last of Jack Clough's 143 consecutive Football League appearances as Bradford's goalkeeper, the sequence having started immediately after he joined the club from Middlesbrough.

DECEMBER

The heaviest player in the club's history was Hugh McDonald, the former Woolwich Arsenal goalkeeper. He made his Bradford debut on December 2, 1911, in an away Second Division match at Grimsby Town. McDonald weighed in at 15st 6lb and stood 6ft 2ins.

On December 3, 1927, Bert Davis made his Football League debut for Bradford at Park Avenue in a Northern Section match against Accrington Stanley. Davis, at 5ft 4ins., was the smallest player who ever appeared with the club until Willie Donaldson (same height) arrived in 1946.

Bradford played their first friendly against overseas opposition on December 4, 1935, when Vienna visited Park Avenue. Bradford won by 3-1 before a crowd of 4,004.

Eddie Parris, Bradford's outside-left, playing for Wales against Ireland on December 5, 1931, became the first coloured player in history to appear in the International Championship.

A wartime representative match at Park Avenue between the FA and The Army attracted 12,688 (£1,500) to the ground on December 9, 1944.

Harold Taylor made the first of his 334 Football League appearances for Bradford on December 10, 1921, in a match against Hull City - a pre-war club record.

Bradford's team against Coventry City at Park Avenue on December 10, 1949, was without a Scot for the first time since February 1, 1936, the side comprising ten Englishmen and an Irishman (Currie). Team: Nicholls; Farrell, Hepworth; White, Horsman, Elliott; Smith, Henry, Currie, Deplidge, Stevens.

New Brompton drew a Southern League game at Park Avenue by 5-5 on December 14, 1907, this after Bradford had held a 5-1 lead.

The smallest derby attendance for a senior match between the wool city rivals was just 575. That was the crowd for a wartime North Regional fixture at Valley Parade on December 14, 1940.

The FA Cup second round on December 15, 1951, paired the Bradford clubs at Park Avenue in an all-ticket tie. The ticket limit was fixed at 29,000, but the crowd was 24,430 (£2,260). Bradford won by 3-2.

Bradford centre-forward Barry Smith registered his fifth hat-trick of 1956 on December 15 when Crewe Alexandra were beaten by 4-3 at Park Avenue in a Northern Section game. In the previous league game two weeks earlier Smith had scored all the Bradford goals in a 3-0 win at Tranmere Rovers.

On December 16, 1950, Alec Horsfield scored for Bradford in eight minutes at Barrow when making his Football League debut four days after being secured from Arsenal with whom he had had no first team chance in over four years.

Bradford chalked up their biggest victory against neighbours City when they netted ten times without reply on December 19, 1942, in a Football League North match at Valley Parade.

Dick Conroy, appearing with Bradford against City at Valley Parade on December 19, 1953, became the first player in history to have represented both clubs in the series of peace-time Football League meetings of the pair.

On Friday, December 20, 1907, Bradford began the longest inland match tour in their history. They stayed Friday night and also Saturday, Sunday and Monday in London after having met Millwall in the Southern League on the Saturday. They travelled to Bristol on the Tuesday to meet Rovers on the following day (Christmas Day), returned to London in the evening for a Boxing Day match with Leyton on the Thursday, and came back to Bradford on the Friday.

Bradford were featured for the first time on television on December 21, 1968, when Yorkshire Television took in the Park Avenue Fourth Division derby with Doncaster Rovers. Bradford won by 2-1.

Bradford's highest-ever Football League attendance was recorded on Christmas Day 1925, when 32,429 watched the Second Division clash with Leeds United.

Arthur Farrell

Goalkeeper Ernald Scattergood converted two penalties in Bradford's 3-1 Second Division home win against Clapton Orient on Boxing Day, 1921.

On Boxing Day, 1959, Archie McHard scored in 12 seconds in a Park Avenue Fourth Division match against Southport. This beat the previous record of 15 seconds set up by Harry McIlvenny on September 24, 1949.

Bradford announced they had suspended Arthur Farrell on December 29, 1950, for a fortnight because of his refusal to play at right-back against Rotherham United at Millmoor on Boxing Day.

Bradford suspended centre-forward Arthur Adey on December 30, 1954, for 14 days after he had twice arrived late at the ground for home matches.

INTO THE UNKNOWN

FIRST MATCH IN THE SOUTHERN LEAGUE

From the Bradford Daily Telegraph of September 9, 1907:

'The Bradford Association Club have made a good beginning to their Southern League fixture by recording a meritorious victory over Reading. It would have occasioned no surprise had the new club only effected a draw after their long journey south but they rose to the occasion grandly."

No score at half-time. Then: "Manning made tracks for goal at great pace. Carrick came up on the other wing to be in readiness and as he was unmarked he had no difficulty on receiving the ball from the right-winger in scoring with a low fast drive.

"This was a success which gave as much delight to the left winger as it did to the members of the Bradford Committee seated on the stand [were they perched on the roof?]. Carrick was desirous of doing well against his old clubmates of Reading and he also felt pleased to have the honour of scoring the first Southern League goal for the club.

In the next couple of minutes Manning "dropped a high ball into goal" (2-0) and then came a brilliant combined move by Bradford. Wood, Mair and M'Kie started it, Manning and Reid joined in and M'Kie's effort to score was pushed out by goalie Rae only for Fisher to "charge down upon it and bang it into the net."

Just before the end Christie tripped Minter to concede a penalty from which Gee scored for Reading.

"The interest taken in the northern club was shown by the large crowd. The Reading team usually attract four to five thousand spectators but the fact that Bradford were the visitors drew an attendance up to 7,000."

THE FIRST MATCH IN THE FOOTBALL LEAGUE

From the Bradford Daily Telegraph of September 2, 1908

"The Bradford Club made a most auspicious beginning with their Second Division fixtures last night and their 1-0 victory over Hull City will go a long way towards establishing them in the favour of the football public of Bradford. They have set their feet on the first rung of the league ladder and if we may judge from last night's performance they are likely to mount many steps higher"

Avenue had a stiff breeze behind them and from a Manning corner Fraser registered the club's first league goal. Manning gave Stephenson, the Hull left-back, a lot of trouble and Donald gave a fine exhibition: neither Browell nor M'Quillan could hold this clever player.

The crowd was between ten and 12 thousand and the gate money amounted to £240.

THE FIRST MATCH IN THE FIRST DIVISION

From the Bradford Daily Telegraph of September 7, 1914

"In making their debut in the First Division on Saturday at Park Avenue Bradford had the good fortune to have as visitors such an attractive side as Blackburn Rovers The champions of the league possess a great team which is skilful both in attack and defence and plays strong and robust football. Bradford relied on the team which gained promotion with the single exception of Stirling, the ex-Middlesbrough player, at outside-right. In the presence of some 25,000 spectators the game started at a great pace and Bauchop opened the scoring after eight minutes, a goal which was cleverly worked for and well deserved."

For half an hour Bradford were the better side and led by that goal at the interval. But "the second half was not far advanced when Blackburn took the lead, Dawson and Shee getting in shots which gave Drabble no chance."

The report suggested that in the second half Bradford's inside men kept the ball too close to the neglect of their wingers. But the Telegraph concluded: "Bradford played a great game against their powerful opponents and the same form maintained against other teams should see them making progress in the league."

THE FIRST GAME IN THE THIRD NORTH

From the Bradford Daily Telegraph of August 26, 1922

"The clerk of the weather had evidently got his seasons hopelessly mixed and the coming of football was greeted by pleasant summer-like weather which at any rate was appreciated by the spectators."

(At Brighton Yorkshire were tumbled out for 42, only Herbert Sutcliffe (12) making double figures. It was a big come-down after a ten-wicket victory against Hampshire at Bournemouth where Wilfred Rhodes scored 108 and Sutcliffe 81 in a total of 293.)

From the Telegraph of August 28: "To David Howie, the captain of the side, fell fittingly the club's first goal in Third Division Football. But the man of the match was undoubtedly Peel. His combination with M'Candless and McLean was always most effective while his individual work was excellent. Shooting was the only weak point in an otherwise splendid display but if he rarely tested the Nelson goalkeeper he saw to it that his colleagues had many scoring chances. And that, after all, is genius. Howie's support of the attack was most effective but under pressure it was McDonald who shone. Not only did he hold his immediate opponents but he found opportunities to lend assistance Fell must have appreciated in keeping Eddleston in check. McGloughlin's vigour and Brandon's coolness and resource should blend into a strong bulwark between opposing attacks and Scattergood."

THE FIRST FOURTH DIVISION MATCH

From the Telegraph & Argus of August 25, 1958

"Bradford did themselves a lot of good (writes Dick Williamson) by the nature of their exhibition in a 3-2 conquest of Workington that should have been bigger and a 9,343 satisfied crowd was evidence that there will be healthy support for Fourth Division football at Park Avenue - if quality football and the right results continue.

"The forward play touched a plane beyond what has been habitual with Avenue in recent years and a goal flow was inevitable from the shrewd scheming of Buchanan whose calculating work was a big factor in those that came from Atkinson and Booth (2), who were assertive and purposeful."

THE FIRST GAME IN THE WEST RIDING COUNTY AMATEUR LEAGUE

From the Telegraph & Argus of September 1, 1988

"Newly re-formed Bradford Park Avenue made a triumphant return to competitive soccer last night (writes Bill Marshall) - 14 years after the club went out of existence.

"A crowd of about 300 saw them defeat Salts Reserves in a home game at Manningham Mills FC in the Third Division of the West Riding County Amateur League. The scene was vastly different from the heady days in the Football League on the famous Park Avenue ground, but the result was a tremendous boost.

"Avenue's opening night hero was substitute Chris McDonald. His goal ten minutes from time proved to be the winner.

"Salts went ahead in the second minute through a Trevor Hardaker header and, although Avenue stormed back, splendid defensive work held them at bay until the break.

"Avenue took charge in the second half with goals from Paul Armitage and Steve Jenson, only for Nicky Griggs to equalise.

"The match was kicked off by former Avenue stalwart Charlie Atkinson."

CLOWN PRINCE REMEMBERED
BY TIM CLAPHAM

I first met Len Shackleton at an Avenue book launch in Bradford during the summer of 1987, when there was only time to exchange a few brief words. Our second meeting was on a fine summer's day at Grange-over-Sands, where the former Bradford, Newcastle, Sunderland and England inside-forward had settled in retirement.

We had arranged the meeting after corresponding over a number of months. Len was eager for me to keep him informed of the happenings at the revived club and I had an important invitation to deliver. Despite relocating to Morecambe Bay, Len had kept in touch with all his old friends, especially those from the world of soccer, and only the previous day he had enjoyed a game of golf at the local course with long-time pal Bob Stokoe, who apparently was a regular visitor.

We talked at length about all things Avenue, and as club historian I was particularly interested to hear stories of his time at Park Avenue during the 1940s. One tale concerned his relationship with Halifax referee Arthur Ellis, who carved out an unlikely career in TV many years later co-presenting a game show. It is well documented that Len did not hold much regard for any kind of officialdom, but in Arthur's case he made an exception. He recalled one occasion when Ellis chose to ignore several remarks from him of "Terrible decision." But, late in the game, Ellis watched Len shoot wide of an open goal, then ran past saying, "Terrible shot!" Both had a good laugh about it after the game.

Looking back to his schooldays, Len told me of the day Avenue manager Billy Hardy called at his home and invited him to join Bradford as an amateur. Although Len was perfectly happy with this and keen to accept, his father had reservations and said it was wrong that his lad should go to Park Avenue when the rest of the family were Bradford City supporters. Thankfully, the objections were overcome.

Len told me he had thoroughly enjoyed his wartime experiences at Park Avenue and, to some extent, his time down the pit as a Bevin Boy at Fryston Colliery, where he worked with Avenue team-mate Jimmy Stephen. However, when Newcastle stepped in with an offer for him he realised it was time to go. He was pleased Bradford had picked up a 'decent payment' for his transfer to Tyneside in 1946, and that this went someway to softening the blow of his departure so soon after peace-time soccer had resumed.

My main reason for visiting Len was to invite him to become an Avenue vice-president and I wasn't disappointed with his reaction. He immediately accepted and promised that his first appearance would be at the club's annual dinner later that year. Before I left I asked him whether he would have changed anything given his time again on the football field, and I am sure I knew the answer before he gave it. He told me that he was always first and foremost an entertainer and it was tough if the powers-that-be didn't like it. He said his fans at Bradford, Newcastle and Sunderland loved him and that was all that mattered.

I saw Len several more times over the next few years, both in Bradford and Grange, and at Kendal, where he was once guest of honour of the Cumbrian club when they hosted Avenue in a UniBond League match. But our friendship sadly came to a close in November 2000 when the final whistle blew for the "Clown Prince."

AUTHORS' NOTE

The death of Len Shackleton in 2000 merited a somewhat unexpected reference in Wisden, the cricketer's bible. It noted that he had played in Minor Counties cricket for Northumberland and Durham. In a Northumberland League match he once scored 117 not out and then took 8-35 with his seamers. He also appeared for Lidget Green in a war-time Bradford League studded with county players like George Pope, Leslie Ames, Len Hutton and Bill Copson.

It is not too widely known that during his playing days Shack undertook a number of soccer coaching tours during the summer to such places as East Africa and Hong Kong.

Len's autobiography, published by GHKN Publishing Ltd just before he died in 2000.

The Fryston Colliery team of 1946, where many young Bradford players worked as Bevin Boys during the war. Back: Joe Mordue, Jimmy Stephen, Arthur Roberts (York City), Donald Maddison, Arthur Farrell, Sam Gledhill (York City). Front: Richard Dix, Jackie Smith, Johnny Downie, Len Shackleton, Geoff Walker

PARK AVENUE AND ME
BY MALC HARTLEY

The oddest experience I ever had at Park Avenue had nothing to do with football - nor even cricket.

It arose during a print strike at the Telegraph & Argus. This stopped production of the newspaper, then selling nearly 120,000 copies a day, but the editorial department continued to function and it was decided we should make a daily summary of local news over the hospital broadcasting system. I was one of three people who took it in turn to do this. The necessary equipment was housed at Park Avenue where members of the Hospital Broadcasting Association did sports commentaries and for some reason I can't remember we were called on to deliver our news from a tiny room somewhere in the heart of the grandstand complex. You called at the club office, collected your gear, made your way to this ill-lit little hidey-hole and, having synchronised your watch with the City Hall clock, plugged in and switched on at exactly 2pm. You then read your prepared bulletin.

The thing is that you were entirely alone. There was no introduction or anything like that, no producer coming through headphones to give you a cue. It was exactly like talking to yourself. I used to wonder whether what I was saying was being heard by anyone or whether I was just sitting in not-so-splendid isolation speaking into a mike as a weird way of passing a few minutes of the afternoon!

It was a complete contrast to broadcasting with Pennine and Radio Leeds as author of football books when I faced an interviewer across the table, each with his own microphone.

My first duties at Avenue were as a young editorial messenger. Another room deep under the stand housed telephones which were used on county cricket days for the dictation of reports to newspaper offices. The Press box was on the other side of the ground by the pavilion where Dick Williamson typed his report as play progressed and it was my job to visit him periodically, collect his "copy," make my way back round the ground and phone what he'd typed to Hall Ings. That was reasonably interesting - until the rain. But some of the most boring times of my life were suffered in that telephone room amid the stench of wet raincoats when rain stopped play. You couldn't leave in case by some miracle play restarted. You had to stand - no seats as I recall - and watch the rain falling steadily and aching for an announcement that play had been abandoned for the day.

My friend Stan Pearson, who later covered the dying days of league football at the ground, once had a hard time as a fellow messenger. You see not only did we have to visit Williamson at regular intervals but also at the fall of each wicket. Stan was on duty the day of the Test trial when Jim Laker took eight wickets for two runs and it was an all-action exercise for Stan who rushed round the ground so often that spectators began to cheer and jeer every time he went past!

On the subject of taking "copy", one of the duties of the reporting staff used to be sitting in built-in telephone kiosks at the side of the newsroom and typing reports phoned from correspondents from a variety of sporting centres on Saturday afternoons for Yorkshire Sports. The one job most of them feared was coping with Dick Williamson. It would be inaccurate to say that he did not suffer fools gladly - he did not put up with fools at all. If he was given an incompetent copytaker he was soon demanding to speak to Vic Thompson, the head copytaker, and insisting on a replacement.

Four or five "outsiders" would come in to earn a few pennies by supplementing staffmen and one in particular had no qualms about taking Dick. He would bawl back at him with gusto: after all he was not in his employment and he could afford to shrug his shoulders if he was not asked to come again.

In due season he disappeared and, with useful experience from "taking" Don Alred at Valley Parade I volunteered to type Avenue reports. Thanks to my interest in and knowledge of football I was better suited to the job than most, gradually established a rapport with Dick and thoroughly enjoyed it. We had our own phone at Park Avenue and Dick left the line open for several minutes at a time so that through my headphones I could hear the crowd, listen to the chatter in the Press box and feel it was the next best thing to being at the match.

Eventually Dick would snap: "Cut it off there" and I would wait for the phone to ring next time. Bear in mind that by no means all the staffmen were sports-minded and you can guess how they struggled with unfamiliar terms, to say nothing of Dick's rasping impatience if he was asked to repeat anything.

I owe Bobby Ham an apology. One year he led my old school, Grange, in the final of the Bradford Schools FA Cup against Highfield and I did the report for the old Yorkshire Observer morning paper. When I saw "Ham" on the programme I thought it must be a misprint. I had heard of Geoff Hamm of Woking, soon to be become an England amateur international, and assumed the programme had missed off an "m". Without checking, I gave Bobby's surname an extra "m" too. Sorry, Bob. It reminds me that when I played at Grange a colleague was Trevor Hammond whose nickname was "Eggs". Hammond Eggs, see? He was a goalkeeper and liked his nickname so much that he cajoled his mother into embroidering his jersey with two eggs.

Another brief mention of that schools final. Man of the match was Bruce Stowell, who went on to captain Bradford City. And the trophy was presented by the Lord Mayor, Alderman Dick Ruth, a dignified and assiduous worker for Bradford City Council whose persistence and determination had much to do with the elevation of Bradford's Institute of Technology to university status. He is commemorated only by a block of flats at the foot of Otley Road called Ruth House and I'm afraid not many now will have any idea of who Ruth was or what a debt the city owes him for his unstinting work for his city in the days before councillors were paid.

As a boy I would collect autographs from players as they left the back of what several books and articles have described as the Doll's House, though I never heard that description applied to the pavilion at the time. Two instances come to mind. Albert Nightingale of Huddersfield Town and later Leeds United, made us stand in orderly line before he would sign anything; but he then stood patiently and gave everyone his autograph. When Southampton came, they were taken back to Exchange Station after the match in taxis. I poked my book through the front window of one of the cars and it was taken by the big centre-forward, Tom Lewis. "Do you want my autograph?" he asked. I said: "You've already signed my book, thank you. I was hoping to have the gentleman in the back". Lewis retorted: "That's no gentleman that's Alf Ramsey." And with the very faintest suggestion of a smile the World Cup-winning manager of the future added his signature to my collection.

Incidentally I still possess the autographs I sought as a teenager and the significant thing is that you can read them all without difficulty. Having been shown a few modern-day "autographs" and seen reproductions of others, I am bound to say that autographs today, even if you can get near the players, are a reminder that peasants used to have their own mark because they could not read or write. Most I have seen are indecipherable squiggles.

In one of my spells as deputy to Dick Williamson I wrote about Avenue at a time when Wally Galbraith was the manager. He was always most charming to me and with his clipped moustache and dark, swept-back hair I guessed he would have no trouble engaging the attention of the fair sex

On a trip to play Hartlepool United he told me that when he had visited the ground as a player he had found the showers to be in such a filthy state that after the game, rather than risk an infection from them he put his clothes on over the caked mud and waited until he arrived home to clean himself properly. I hasten to add that the Hartlepools' ground has long since been completely modernised and I'm sure there are no complaints now about facilities.

The Park Avenue sports complex is no longer there but for 60 years it was the local theatre of sporting dreams. All the leading players appeared on the cricket ground which was renowned for a sporting wicket. On the football side thousands upon thousands of people from the city and surrounding towns cheered, jeered, applauded, groaned and experienced the roller-coaster of spiralling excitement and tumbling despair.

The team, especially when wearing their unique red, amber and black shirts, gave us colour. But think of this: if the main stand had lived to celebrate its centenary, the health and safety regulators would have put an end to it anyway.

AUTHORS' NOTE

Malc Hartley spent all his working life at on the Telegraph & Argus and associated newspapers in Bradford and was deputy football writer to Williamson and Don Alred, who covered Bradford City. Williamson reported on Park Avenue football and county cricket and became editor of "Yorkshire Sports."

Park Avenue in various states of decay and demolition.

Authors Hartley and Clapham pictured by Mrs Rosemary Hartley at Horsfall Stadium when Avenue fist moved to the ground. Malcolm is wearing red, amber and black hoops and Tim the white and green shirt of the time.

SHORTS

CUP FIGHTERS

Although Avenue never made it to Wembley they did appear in the FA Cup quarter-finals three times.

The first occasion was in 1913 as Second Division mid-tablers when they beat Barrow 1-0 after a 1-1 draw (both ties played at Park Avenue by mutual agreement), Wolves 3-0 at home and Sheffield Wednesday (First Division title challengers) 2-1 at home. Then they were given a hefty boot, 5-0 by the eventual winners, Aston Villa.

In 1920, by now mid-tablers in the First Division, they knocked out Nottingham Forest 3-0, Midland Leaguers Castleford Town 3-2, won 4-3 away to Notts County (fellow members of the First Division) and then fell 4-1 away to Chelsea. Chelsea were then beaten by Aston Villa, who lifted the trophy again.

In 1945-6 when the FA Cup resumed after the war ties were played over two legs. Bradford disposed of Port Vale (2-1, 1-1), Second Division champions-elect Manchester City (1-3 at Avenue, a sensational 8-2 at Maine Road) and Barnsley (1-0, 1-1) before succumbing to Birmingham 2-2 at home but 6-0 at St Andrew's.

1913 - Bob Mason; Alex Watson, Sam Blackham; George Halley, Bert Dainty, Jack Scott; Danny Munro, Tommy Little, Jimmy Smith (five goals), David Howie and Willie Kivlichan.

1920 - Ernie Scattergood; Sam Blackham, Wally Dickenson; Joe Crozier, David Howie, Jack Scott; Bob Turnbull, Tommy Little, David McLean (five goals), Jimmy Bauchop and Jack McCandless.

1946 - Chick Farr; Ronnie Hepworth, Arthur Farrell; Ron Greenwood, Bob Danskin, Bill Hallard; Jackie Smith/Bert Knott, Len Shackleton, Jack Gibbons (eight goals), Johnny Downie and Richard Dix/Geoff Walker.

WINGING ROUND THE WORLD

Bradford winger Bob Turnbull was selected for the FA party to tour South Africa in 1920. The squad won all their 14 games with goal figures of 64-10, Turnbull contributing six. They sailed from Southampton aboard the SS Briton on Friday May 7, arriving at Cape Town on May 28 for a civic reception. Leading scorer on the tour was Joe Smith of Bolton, later manager of Blackpool when they won the cup in 1953.

Turnbull made a second tour of South Africa with the FA in 1929, by which time he was with Leeds United. He represented England in three victory internationals in 1919 and received a full cap against Ireland in October that year with Joe Smith at inside-left.

Bob Turnbull takes a free-kick in front of the Doll's House at Park Avenue

Another Avenue winger who had a travelling experience to remember was Ronnie Bird, the penalty king - 14 for the club in the early 1960s. He joined Jimmy Scoular after the Scot had taken the reins at Cardiff City and in 1967-8 they had an adventure in fulfilling a European Cup-winner's Cup quarter-final against Moscow Torpedo.

After securing the only goal in the first leg at Ninian Park they set out for the return, only to arrive in Moscow in sub-zero temperatures to find the pitch under nine feet of snow in places. Play was clearly out of the question and Torpedo switched the venue to what they called their summer ground at Tashkent, capital of Uzbekistan - which was 2,000 miles away from Moscow and only 300 miles from China!

Cardiff did well to lose by only 1-0 (meaning a replay) and then came the inordinately long haul back to the UK. They arrived home after almost a week on travel having covered some 7,000 miles - the longest journey ever made to fulfil a European tie. Cardiff won the replay 1-0 in Germany but were beaten in the semi-finals by SV Hamburg.

A third Bradford winger who played in a faraway place was dapper Les Stevens, signed from Spurs in February 1949.

He graduated from the ground staff at White Hart Lane and impressed Avenue with his performance against them in 1947 which brought to an end their six-wins-in-a-row start.

During the war he volunteered for the RAF as soon as he was old enough and was sent across the Atlantic to Canada. From this base he played football on tour in America with a Services team.

A Londoner from Croydon who represented Croydon and Surrey Boys, he guested for five London clubs before peace returned and he left Avenue to join one of them, Crystal Palace, in 1950.

Les Stevens

VINTAGE CLARET

Right-half in the first Bradford team to make an impact in the FA Cup was George Halley, who went on to become part of the legendary Halley, Boyle 'n' Watson middle line which helped the club set up a Football League record of 30 matches without defeat in 1920-1.

He went to Turf Moor for £1,200 in March 1913 and straight away helped Burnley to the semi-final and promotion to the First Division. In 1914 he was in the only Burnley team ever to win the FA Cup and they did it in the first final to be watched by the reigning monarch, King George V.

They were captained by Tommy Boyle. Billy Taylor was then the left-half and the significant forward was Bert Freeman who scored the only goal but had been the league's top scorer the two previous seasons.

Halley volunteered for the Forces and saw out postings to India and Mesopotamia.

After three games of 1920-1 Burnley were bottom of Division One but by now they had Bob Kelly, one of the greatest inside-forwards ever seen in the Football League, in the attack and by autumn the Clarets were challenging for the championship.

Halley played in the first 23 of Burnley's record 30 league matches without defeat before having to drop out suffering from pneumonia. His team went on to the championship so the former Avenue half-back had earned cup-winner's and league championship medals.

Today's record unbeaten sequence of 49 by Arsenal spans three seasons - from May 7, 2003 to October 2004.

RESERVES' GOAL ACE

Trevor Rhodes had the highly satisfactory - you would think - goal haul of 39 in 57 Second Division matches for Avenue yet he could never pin down the centre-forward position.

He made his debut in 1928-9 and his best season was 1930-1 when Bradford finished sixth and Rhodes was top scorer with 19 in 21 games.

He forced his way into the team with an unparalleled feat - he scored six goals or more in a match for the club in three different competitions: six against Burnley reserves in the Northern Midweek League in November 1929; seven against Newark Town in the Midland League in September 1931; and eight against Frickley Colliery also in the Midland League, in October 1931.

Port Vale, who were companions with Avenue in the Second Division, were pleased to obtain his transfer in the close season of 1933 and he became a first-team regular at inside-right, dropping back to right-half in 1936-7. He scored 28 in 140 matches before losing his place through injury in November 1937.

In his first two seasons with Vale the team's top scorer was Tommy Nolan, who came to Park Avenue in 1935 and led Avenue's list in his first season. And towards the end of Rhodes's days in the Vale a team-mate was George Stabb, who followed Nolan to Avenue and stayed for many years, first as a player and then on the training staff. Rhodes was born at Leeds and died there in 1993.

SAINTS SENT PACKING

Avenue's favourite visitors in the 1930s were Southampton. From their return to the Second Division in 1928 to the outbreak of war Bradford beat the Saints nine times at Park Avenue and drew the other two. From 1931 they won eight in a row at home. Over the same period Bradford's record at The Dell was won 2, drawn 3, lost 6.

FAMOUS NAMES

Alex James, long-shorted Scottish midfield maestro of Arsenal's great team of the 1930s, played at Park Avenue for Preston North End on October 27, 1928. Promoted Avenue won 7-2. By the time Preston next visited Avenue in March 1930 James was well on his way to his first cup-winner's medal with Arsenal.

Peter Doherty, non-stop Irish legend, made his Football League debut at Park Avenue for Blackpool on December 23, 1933.

Dave Whelan, millionaire owner of Wigan Athletic, was born in Bradford at 9 Airedale College Terrace, off Otley Road.

Stanley Matthews played at Park Avenue in two cup matches. In January 1938 he was with Stoke City for a fourth round visit seen by 31,347 and in April 1944 he helped draw Bradford's record attendance of 32,814 when he played for Blackpool as a wartime guest in the quarter-finals of the League North Cup.

Have you seen the well-to-do
Up and down Park Avenue
On that famous thoroughfare
With their noses in the air?
Irving Berlin (Putting on the Ritz)

BETWEEN OUR-SHELVES

In addition to Len Shackleton who put his name to two books and was the subject of two others, Ron Greenwood was another former Avenue man who contributed to football literature with his 240-page hardback "Yours Sincerely" in 1984.

But there's a third much less known former Bradford footballer who committed his thoughts to print, taking a different aspect.

Malcolm Cook, a Glaswegian who was brought to Bradford from Motherwell by Jimmy Scoular in 1963, suffered a knee injury while with Newport which ended his playing career at the age of 23.

He turned to coaching and school-teaching, became a full-badge FA coach and was youth team coach for Doncaster Rovers for a spell after teaching at Princeville Middle School in Bradford.

He was physical education teacher at Thornton Upper when Kenny Dalglish invited him to join the Anfield staff as youth development officer in August 1986 and subsequently published (with Nick Whitehead) a book "Soccer Training" which went through a number of editions.

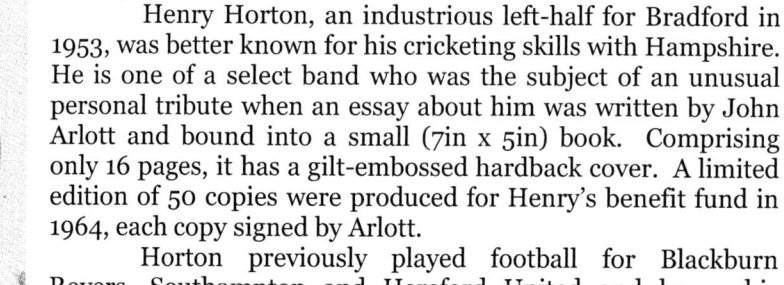

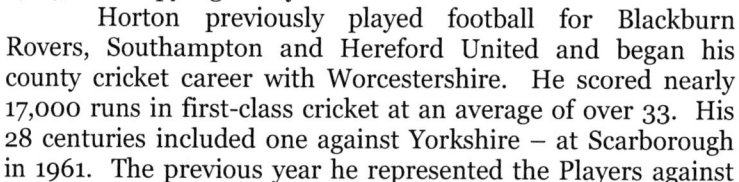

Henry Horton, an industrious left-half for Bradford in 1953, was better known for his cricketing skills with Hampshire. He is one of a select band who was the subject of an unusual personal tribute when an essay about him was written by John Arlott and bound into a small (7in x 5in) book. Comprising only 16 pages, it has a gilt-embossed hardback cover. A limited edition of 50 copies were produced for Henry's benefit fund in 1964, each copy signed by Arlott.

Horton previously played football for Blackburn Rovers, Southampton and Hereford United and began his county cricket career with Worcestershire. He scored nearly 17,000 runs in first-class cricket at an average of over 33. His 28 centuries included one against Yorkshire – at Scarborough in 1961. The previous year he represented the Players against the Gentlemen at Lord's in what was then a prestige annual fixture.

Henry Horton

His sporting highlight was 1962 when he batted no. 3 in helping Hampshire win the county cricket championship for the first time in their history.

The brilliantly-designed hardback book, "The Avenue" compiled by Malcolm Hartley and Tim Clapham and published in 1987, had some remarkable consequences.

In the first place it was the best seller at W H Smith Broadway over six months, being bought more eagerly than a book by Geoffrey Boycott and another by Stephen King.

Then it triggered the enthusiasm of Bob Robinson to restart the club which had folded in 1974 and which subsequently enjoyed several promotions through the non-league pyramid system.

And it became a collector's item to the point where it began to change hands for £100 per copy! As it had been a sell-out and the publishers declined to do a reprint, its scarcity value drove up its second-hand price into three figures.

Whether its value was affected by "All About Avenue", published in 2004, is not known. This second Hartley-Clapham book is a splendidly comprehensive look at leading players, club records, odd happenings and a definitive statistical list of every Football League season with scorers, attendances and teams. Copies are still available for £14 from the publisher Tony Brown at the address at the front of this book.

MORE SHORTS

The Bradford team which defeated Partizan Belgrade 2-0 in a Festival of Britain match in May 1951 was Mitch Downie; Suddards, Hindle; Lynn, Horsman, Deplidge; Smith Hodgson, Crosbie, Haines and Elliott. The Yugoslavs, who included two players who had opposed England the previous November (2-2 at Highbury) were fresh from victories against Middlesbrough (sixth in the First Division) and Hull City (tenth in the second).

From "The Yorkshire Observer" of May 9, 1921: "The Football League authorities would do well during the close season to take steps to put some check on transfer fees which are soaring to a ridiculous height. The latest reported offer of £6,000 for Frank Barson the Aston Villa centre-half is about the limit in this mad bidding for players. No wonder there is unrest among the players when they see clubs paying such huge sums and their own share is strictly limited."

The record attendance for an FA Cup-tie at Park Avenue was 31,347 against First Division Stoke City, Matthews and all, on January 22, 1938. On five other occasions there were more than 30,000 in the ground.

Gifts from the Supporters' Club and Bradford Sportsmen's Association totalling £14,383 exceeded Bradford Football Club's entire gate receipts of £13,478 in 1958-9.

In April 1960 Avenue fielded eight Scots for the first time in a Football League match against Northampton, the line-up being Harry Hough; Jimmy Walker, Watty Dick; Don Brims, Don McCalman, Charlie Atkinson; Ian Gibson, Jock Buchanan, John Allan, Felix Reilly, Ray Byrom.

Bobby Simpson

But in February 1912 they had gone one better in a cup match against Bradford City when Avenue were represented by nine Scots plus Sam Blackham and Herbert Dainty. The team was Hugh McDonald; Alex Watson, Blackham; George Halley, Dainty, Jack Scott; Willie Kivlichan, Jimmy Turnbull, Bobby Simpson, David Howie and Dan Munro.

Sunderland (in 1902) turned out an all-Scottish team against Liverpool, as did Accrington Stanley against York City in April 1955. In this Third North encounter the Accrington goalkeeper was Tom McQueen, whose son Gordon became an international Leeds United defender.

In December 1999 Chelsea became the first English club to field a team which contained no British players. It comprised Ed De Goey (Holland); Albert Ferrer (Spain), Emerson Thome (Brazil), Frank Leboeuf (France), Celestine Babayaro (Nigeria); Dan Petrescu (Rumania), Didier Deschamps (France), Robert Di Matteo (Italy), Gabrielle Ambrosetti (Italy), Gustavo Poyet (Uruguay) and Tore Andre Flo (Norway), who scored both goals in a 2-1 win at Southampton

Matt Crowe, who played one match for Bradford in a 1-0 home defeat against Chesterfield at the end of January 1953, went on to become a regular member of Norwich City's Third South team of 1958-9 which captivated football fans everywhere by reaching the FA Cup semi-finals.

He was the regular left-half as the Canaries toppled Manchester United, Spurs and Sheffield United before falling to First Division Luton Town 1-0 in a semi-final replay. Matt finished up in South Africa managing Port Elizabeth.

Irishman Charlie Heffron, who kept goal 25 times for Avenue in the Third North during 1951 and 1952, won an Irish Cup winner's medal with Derry City in 1954.

The team's achievement was notable for the fact that in the forward line was Jimmy Delaney who added an Irish medal to his Scottish Cup winner's medal earned with Celtic in 1937 and an FA Cup winner's medal collected with Manchester United in 1948.

Derry beat Glentoran 1-0 after two drawn ties. Two years later Delaney figured in a fourth country's cup final with Cork Athletic but they fell to Shamrock Rovers.

During the 1950s Bradford went through seven managers in just over seven years:

Fred Emery	Nov 1943	June 1951
Vic Buckingham	June 1951	Jan 1953
Norman Kirkman	Mar 1953	Dec 1954
Jack Breedon	Jan 1955	Oct 1955
Bill Corkhill	May 1956	Nov 1957
Alf Young	Dec 1957	Nov 1958
Walter Galbraith	Nov 1958	Jan 1961

A CRUSH ON CREWE

In December 1950, Avenue centre-forward Bob Crosbie opened the scoring at Crewe in three minutes, scored another before half-time and finished with a hat-trick in a 4-2 victory. In November 1951 he returned to Gresty Road, claimed another before the break and once more finished with three out of four (result 4-3).

PICK OF THE ATTACK

Eleven players scored four or more in a Football League match for Bradford. One of them was Len Pickard against Accrington Stanley on October 31, 1953, only his third match for the club. His helpmates on the wing were Dennis Brickley and Colin Whitaker.

Pickard followed the route march of Harold Blackmore who graduated all the way from Devon to Yorkshire to score goals at Park Avenue.

Blackmore came from Silverton three miles off what is now the M5 in South Devon; Pickard from Barnstaple on the North Devon coast.

Blackmore netted 32 for Avenue in 60 league games 1933-5; Pickard 31 in 76 1953-6. Len captained Devon schools and was a champion athlete as a young man. He turned out for Barnstaple Town and was with both Bristol clubs before Avenue brought him north and he then returned to the South-west to join Bath City and then Bideford as player-manager.

Other post-war four-goal Avenue men were Jack Gibbons (v Coventry, March 1947), Billy Elliott (in the opening Third North game v Barrow, August 1950), Kenny Booth (at Gateshead September 1958), Jock Buchanan (v Palace, February 1959), Kevin Hector (five v Barnsley November 1965) and Bobby Ham (v Newport, February 1966).

ON THE YORKSHIRE ROUNDABOUT

During 1949-50 chunky inside-right Gerry Henry lost his place in Avenue's first team and joined Sheffield Wednesday. Bradford were relegated while Henry played in Wednesday's last 14 matches, of which only two were lost, and helped them to promotion to the First Division.

In 1952 he was manager of Halifax Town when they enjoyed a famous cup run, seeing off Ashton United, Southport, Cardiff and Stoke City before drawing a plum home tie against Spurs which filled The Shay with 36,885 to see Town's gallant effort ended by a 3-0 margin.

Henry was apparently an uncle by marriage of TV chat show host Michael Parkinson and for 24 years he was mine host at the White Horse at Gomersal.

He spent all his career in his native Yorkshire, moving from Leeds United to Bradford, then to Wednesday and finishing at Halifax. But he played more times for Avenue than any of the other three clubs.

Town's trainer in Henry's time was Alan Ure, who previously filled that position at Park Avenue. He earlier held training posts with Huddersfield, Leeds, Blackpool and Millwall and was manager for one unhappy season at Gillingham (1937-8) when they finished bottom of the Third South and lost their league place to Ipswich Town.

PLANE TO PLAINMOOR

Bradford travelled to a Football League match by air in September 1961, a party of 15 leaving Yeadon for Exeter and then taking a coach to Plainmoor for the fixture against Torquay United. They also flew back to Bradford.

Up to 1957 teams were banned from flying to or from league matches because of insurance problems and potential weather hazards.

In March 1957 Chelsea successfully applied for permission to fly back to London from Newcastle after their Good Friday game; but the first team to fly TO a Football

League fixture were Blackpool, Stanley Matthews et al, who travelled by air the same day for the match against Arsenal at Highbury.

UPWARDLY MOBILE

At 5ft 10in, Colin Whitaker was tall for a winger but arguably Avenue's best outside-left since the elusive Geoff Walker. He was one of those all-round sportsmen who excelled at any ball game.

A fine cricketer, he opened the bowling for Pudsey St Lawrence in the strong Bradford League, was good enough to be invited by Sussex for a trial at Hove and played minor county cricket for Shropshire. He loved golf and had a single figure handicap.

Whitaker left Bradford for Shrewsbury in the summer of 1956 and was a key figure in helping player-manager Arthur Rowley take them to promotion from Division Four in 1958-9. League record scorer Rowley hit 38 goals in 43 matches and Whitaker added 15 as an ever-present.

Neither did he miss a match in his only – and memorable – season at Rochdale. In 1961-2 they reached the League Cup final in the second season of the competition by knocking out First Division Blackburn Rovers but lost the final over two legs to Second Division Norwich City.

He helped Oldham Athletic to promotion the following season and was second-top scorer with 17 in 33 games – a high return from the wing.

Other Avenue players who went on to big things elsewhere include:

Matt Crowe: Left-half in the Norwich City team which, though in the Third Division, reached the FA Cup semi-finals in 1959 and were promoted the following season.
Johnny Downie: First Division championship medal with Manchester United 1952.
Billy Elliott: England, Burnley and Sunderland.
Ian Gibson: Second Division championship medal with Coventry 1967.
Ron Greenwood: First Division championship medal with Chelsea 1955, manager of West Ham and England
Kevin Hector: England sub, many honours with Brian Clough's Derby County.
Paddy Kenny: Premiership with Sheffield United.
Kenny Hibbitt: First Bradfordian to score at Wembley when he helped Wolves win the League Cup in 1974; Fairs Cup finalist in 1972.
Ken Jones: Full-back who made seven appearances for Southampton when they were First Division runners-up in 1966.
Derek Kevan: World Cup games for England in 1958 after joining West Bromwich Albion; joint top-scorer in First Division 1961-2 with 33.
David Lawson: In goal when Everton won League Cup in 1977
Len Shackleton: England caps, semi-finalist and immortal character with Sunderland
Jimmy Stephen: Joined Portsmouth in the First Division
Geoff Walker: Joined Middlesbrough in First Division

Pre-war:
Jack Crayston: England, championship and cup medals with Arsenal
Bert Davis: First Division championship medal with Sunderland 1936
Albert Geldard: England caps, cup winner's medal with Everton 1933
George Halley: Cup and championship medals with Burnley
George McLean: Top scorer when Huddersfield Town were First Division runners-up in 1934
Walter Millership: Cup winner's medal with Sheffield Wednesday 1935
Harold Peel: First Division with Arsenal 1926-9
Jock Wightman: First Division with Huddersfield Town 1934-6

AMBITIOUS QUEST

In the close season of 1950 Bradford officially expressed interest in signing Charlie Wayman, who had been top scorer for Southampton three seasons in a row - 73 goals in 100 Second Division appearances. Instead he joined Preston North End and immediately helped them to the Second Division championship with 27 goals. He was also a member of their cup final team in 1954.

AMONG ENGLAND'S TOP TEN

Bradford's finest team (presumably) was the one that finished ninth in the First Division of 1914-15. Their points total was today's equivalent of 58, which earned Everton sixth place in the Premiership in 2006-07.

Scattergood saves a City attack at Valley Parade, early 1920s

Ernald Scattergood, who turned out 268 times for Avenue, continued the club's early liking for small goalkeepers. Standing only 5ft 8in., he succeeded Baddeley (5ft 9in.) and Mason (5ft 6in.) – and this in the days when the laws of the game allowed him to be charged while holding the ball by heavy forwards.

He held an England cap against Wales (March 1913) and a Second Division championship medal (Derby County 1911-12).

Right-back Alex Watson was one of four Scots in the team (born Stirling) but his partner, the hard-kicking Sam Blackham (221 appearances) came from north London.

Between right-half Joe Crozier, a Middlesbrough man, and Scott the Scot was centre-half and captain David Howie, who made 306 appearances for the club. Jack Scott was born at Motherwell, stayed until June 1921 when he was transferred to Manchester United and went on to foreshadow a custom of 60 years later by joining New York Giants (though under 5ft 9 in. in height!)

Outside-right Jock Stirling from Clydebank had been a Middlesbrough regular.

There was an all-star inside-forward trio. East Londoner Tommy Little began his career as an Ilford amateur and in nine seasons at Avenue (1908-20) cracked 108 goals in 231 League matches, being top scorer in 1911 and 1913.

Centre-forward Jimmy Smith netted 49 in 90 but lost his life near the end of the 1914-18 War to widespread sadness in the city.

Inside-left Jimmy Bauchop was top scorer with 28. He had served Derby County and Spurs before arriving at Park Avenue in 1913, stayed until 1922 and was credited with 157 appearances and 67 goals. He remained in the city and died there in 1948. He was a team-mate of Scattergood when Derby were Second Division champions in 1912.

The remarkable thing about the First Division team was that the tallest member was the Irish outside-left, Jack McCandless, an inch under 6ft.

AUTOGRAPHS

A page of player autographs from the 1930s, with Len Shackleton's added later!

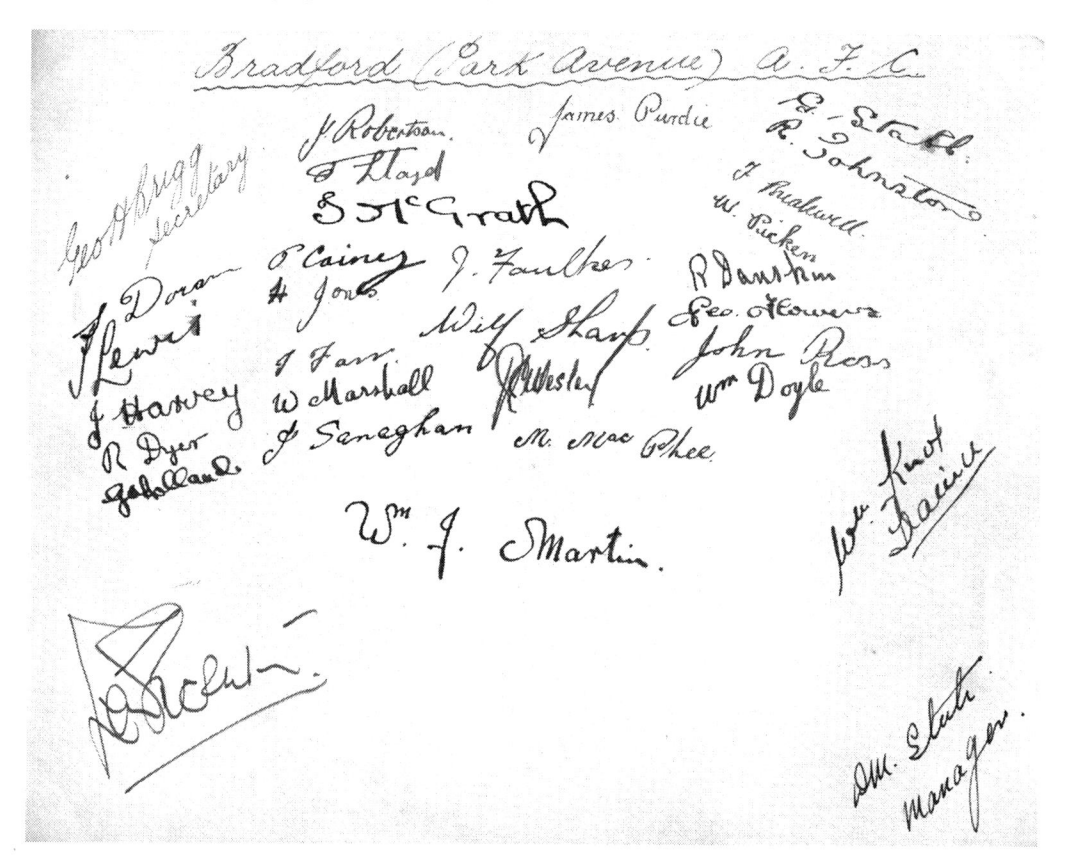

... and some from the 1950s:

BRADFORD (PARK AVENUE) A. F. C.

PLAYING STAFF — SEASON 1950/51

WHAT'S IN A NAME?

Players ready for other trades:

Gerry BAKER (1957-60)
Arthur COLEMAN (1932)
Mal COOK (1963-5)
Derek DRAPER (1967-9)
Bob MASON (1909-14)
Alec GLOVER (1948-9)
Sammy SHEARER (1913)
Jackie SMITH (1946-53)
Graham TANNER (1967-8)
Brian TAYLOR (1954-6)

Colourful players:

Sam BLACKham (1911-22)
Laurie BROWN (1968-9)
George GREEN (1937)
Brian REDfearn (1953-7)
Roy WHITE (1946-50)

Players who could fly:

Ronnie BIRD (1961-4)
Matt CROWE (1953)
Leo PEACOCK (1925)

Players with food connections:

Mal COOK (1963-5)
Charlie CURRIE (1949-54)
Andy HADDOCK (1967-8)
Bobby HAM (1962-8)
Tommy SPRATT (1961-4)
Arthur WHEAT (1950-1)

Players who liked cars:

Alec BENTLEY (1929-31)
Graham CARR (1969-70)
Jim PARKER (1913)
Trevor RHODES (1929-33)
Finlay SPEEDIE (1909)

Players in places of worship:

Edgar BATT (1926-7)
Gary CHURCH (1963
Jack BELL (1931-6}
Harold PEEL (1921-6)
Joby DEAN (1957-8)
Jack WESLEY (1934-7)

Players with geographical names:

Harry BEDFORD (1932-3)
George BLACKBURN (1909-10)
Hugh BOLTON (1909)
Keith FEATHERSTONE (1955)
Peter FRANCE (1957-8)
Tricky HAWES (1927-9)
Jimmy KELSO (1933-4)
Henry HORTON (1954-5)
Ken TEWKESBURY (1935-6)

Players whose surnames are also Christian names:

Alan ALEXANDER (1961-2)
John ALLAN (1959-61)
Ron BRUCE (1938)
Wattie DICK (1958-62)
Davie DONALD (1908-10)
Cliff GODFREY (1929-35)
Alec GORDON 1965-7)
Alex GRAHAM {1937-8)
Kevin HECTOR (1962-6)
Gerry HENRY (1947-50)
Doug HUMPHREY (1921)
Stan JAMES (1950-1)
Derek KEVAN (1952-3)
Harry LEONARD (1947)
Tommy LLOYD (1927-37)
Billy NEIL (1946)
Jimmy STEPHEN (1946-9)
Geoff THOMAS (1963-6)

Country-lovers:

Gerald FELL (1922-7)
Fred FIELD (1934)
Ronnie BIRD (1961-4)
David DOWN (1967-8)
George FLOWERS (1936-7)
Willie HAWTHORN (1933-4)
Jimmy WALKER (1959-63)
Billy WOODS (1947)

Longest Name:

Tommy POSTLETHWAITE (1934-5)

Dates are the calendar years in which the players made league appearances for Bradford.

WHAT'S IN A DATE? – SHARED BIRTHDAYS

Charlie Atkinson	Dec 17	Kerry Packer	Cricket
		Tommy Steele	Entertainer
Pete Brannan	April 7	Sir David Frost	Television
		Cliff Morgan	Rugby/media
		Andrew Sachs	Fawlty Towers
John Brodie	June 8	Nancy Sinatra	Singer
		Ray Illingworth	Cricket
		Colin Baker	Dr Who
		Derek Underwood	Kent/Bankfoot bowler
Terry Dolan	June 11	Jacques Cousteau	Underwater explorer
		Jackie Stewart	Motor racing
		Richard Todd	Film star
		Rachel Heyhoe Flint	Cricket
Peter Flynn	Oct 11	Bobby Charlton	Football
		Maria Bueno	Tennis
		'Mighty Mike' Edwards	Ex supremo BL/ICI
Jim Fryatt	Sep 2	Jimmy Connors	Tennis
		Bob Crosbie	Another Avenue cf
Bert Gebbie	Nov 18	George Gallup	Opinion polls
		Kim Wilde	Singer
		Alec Issigonis	Mini designer
Steve Gibson	May 2	David Beckham	Footballer
		Bing Crosby	Crooner
Bobby Ham	Mar 29	Julie Goodyear	Coronation Street
		Pearl Bailey	Singer
		Eric Idle	Monty Python
		Richard Rodney Bennett	Conductor/composer
Frank Hindle	Jun 22	Meryl Streep	Actor
		Joe Loss	Band leader
		Esther Rantzen	Television
		Mick Kinane	Jockey
Paul I'anson	May 3	Len Shackleton	Clown prince
		Henry Cooper	Boxer
		Alan Wells	Olympic sprinter
Don McCalman	Oct 18	Martina Navratilova	Tennis
		Chuck Berry	R & B
Denis Miles	Aug 6	Frank Finlay	Actor
		Robert Mitchum	Film star
		Barbara Windsor	Actor
		Chris Bonington	Mountaineer
Jim Nicholls	Nov 27	Ernie Wise	Comedian
		Michael Yardy	Sussex/England cricketer
Brian Redfearn	Feb 20	Gordon Brown	Prime Minister
		Jimmy Greaves	Footballer
Ron Routledge	Oct 14	Steve Cram	Athlete
		Roger Moore	James Bond
Alan Tewley	Jan 22	Alf Ramsey	Football
		George Foreman	Boxer
Jimmy Walker	Aug 25	Sean Connery	James Bond
		Frederick Forsyth	Novelist
		Van Johnson	Film star
Polly Ward	June 15	John Redwood	Politician
		Simon Callow	Hi-de-hi!

MAGAZINE MUSINGS 1948-1967

"Sport" magazine (September 4, 1948): Fans at Park Avenue will be delighted to know that Jimmy Stephen, the international full-back, is now out of the RAF and back in the pit.
(out of the frying pan...?)

"Sporting Mirror" (November 1948): Joe Shaw, Arsenal's Chief Scout, was watching several Bradford players last week. His chief interest was in forwards Downie and Ainsley who have scored 19 between them this season but I don't think even Arsenal could tempt Bradford to part with them.

"Sporting Mirror" (March 1949): Many attempts have been made to sign Johnny Downie. Bradford's inside-left, this season. Chelsea were reported to have offered £15,000 and Portsmouth have made persistent inquiries but I understand that a recent bid, nearly the highest ever, is likely to succeed.

"Sport" (October 1949): Once again Jimmy Stephen, who is due for release from the RAF in a short time, has contacted the Park Avenue club about a transfer. I doubt whether the international full-back will re-sign for the club when available for full-time soccer again. Chelsea have offered around £10,000 but Bradford value Stephen higher than that figure.

"Sporting Mirror" (November 1949); Since the middle of the war Bradford have transferred eight players for fees totalling something like £90,000. Stephen (Portsmouth) brought £15,000, Geoff Walker (Middlesbrough) £6,000, Len Shackleton (Newcastle) £13,500, Jack Gibbons.(Brentford) £10,000, George Wilkins (Nottingham Forest) £7,500, Ron Greenwood (Brentford) £9,000, Johnny Downie (Manchester United) £18,000 and Alec Glover (Luton Town) £8,250. The "buys" - Wilkins, Layton, Glover, Crosbie, Currie and Stevens total something like £45,000, which makes quite a handy little profit of £45,000. Yet Bradford are still "the club the soccer boom passed by."

Leon Leuty

"Sport" (January 1950): Biggest shock bar none in the third round of the FA Cup was provided by Bournemouth at Park Avenue where a late goal by Jack Cross enabled the Cherries to beat their Second Division opponents. Territorially Bradford did enough to win hands down but an unusually large crowd (19,709) saw them thwarted by the ultra-brilliance of Boscombe goalkeeper Ken Bird who repelled the repeated advances of Jack Haines and his forward colleagues.

"Sport" (September 1950): Bradford's comfortable win over Southport lifted the Yorkshire side into a useful position to challenge the divisional leaders. Fred Emery's team boasts an abundance of talent rarely seen in the Northern Section and Bradford's early return to Division Two would not cause great surprise in northern circles. But if the Park Avenue boys begin to slide, be prepared for a general scramble for the transfer of Leon Leuty, the former Derby County centre-half.

"Sport" (January 1951): Bradford have not had the best of luck with the star players they have signed and there has been a tendency for men of repute to drift from the Park Avenue fold. Happily we can point to inside-right Jack Haines as a player who has been content to pull his weight in the multi-coloured Bradford shirt without agitating for a move to more glamorous surroundings. Jack can claim an England appearance against Switzerland at Highbury in 1948.

"Soccer Star" (February 1962): There are club chiefs who usually show a marked preference when signing players for nationalities of their own country. That charge certainly cannot be levelled against Bradford player-manager Jimmy Scoular for in the 12 months he has been doing the job nearly all the new players recruited have been Englishmen and nearly all he has transferred have been fellow Scots.

"Soccer Star" (March 1962): Imagine it - only 22 yet a "veteran" sufficient to have been with the same club under SIX managers! That is the strange story of hefty right-back Gerry Baker. Since he began with Bradford, his only club, they have been managed by Norman Kirkman, Jack Breedon, Bill Corkhill, Alf Young, Walter Galbraith and now Jimmy Scoular.

"Soccer Star" (September 1967): Bradford have made some mystifying decisions in the past few months but surely none so odd in cancelling the contract of inside-forward Peter Deakin, who promptly re-signed for Peterborough - the club that had transferred him to Bradford for £4,000 only a year before! Formerly of Bolton Wanderers, Deakin has had a short stay at Bradford and his departure means that the two men signed to fill the gap created by Hector's departure made 61 appearances between them for £12,000. The other was Bobby Waddell, given a free transfer after four goals in 21 games after being signed from Blackpool for £8,000.

Hold the front page! An issue of the weekly "Sport" magazine from March 1948. At the back: Henry, White, Hepworth, Farr, Farrell, Downie. Front: Smith, Ainsley, Greenwood, Elliott, Deplidge

ALWAYS GOOD VALUE

PROGRAMMES THROUGH THE YEARS

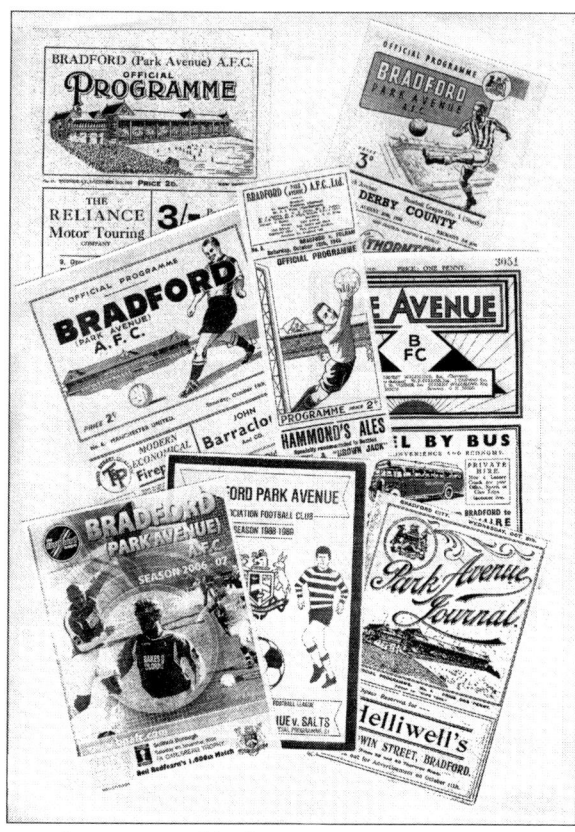

One creditable aspect of Bradford Park Avenue FC is that they have always produced a good programme – and that includes recent times when their issues for non-League games must be the envy of many opponents.

The programme has, of course, shown many changes over the past 100 years. Early issues were rather flimsy affairs but there was a marked improvement when Tom Maley arrived as secretary-manager. After a series of different sized programmes the club settled on an eight-page issue which included comment, fixture lists, Supporters' Club notes and League tables. And for twopence it was good value for money.

Even in the early days the cover was decorated by a nice sketch of the ground and at the start of the 1930s a large size (7in x 10in) programme had a cover sporting a fine photograph of the full length of the main stand. The club telephone number was Bradford 1463!

Advertisers included travel organisers Dean and Dawson; builders Kitching and Hodgson; Knutton's outfitters in Town Hall Square; Gamble and Shapcott, joiners and shop fitters; Skelton's menswear in Market Street; Moffat and Saunders, tobacconists; and Austins from Central Garage right in the middle of the city at Town Hall Square.

During the decade there were "Avenue cameos" of home players. New advertisers included Wil-be-Fort raincoats opposite the New Vic; Greenfield greyhounds, Dudley Hill; Spinks restaurant and bar; Claremont Garage in Morley Street, Joseph Hey's Gold Cup ales, and Scurrahs of Bankfoot ("the radio specialists").

In 1935 there was a dazzling cover in red, yellow and black but this was suspended for one edition: on January 25, for the visit of West Bromwich, the cover was a sober black and white out of respect for King George V, who had just died. Words from "Abide with me" were printed so that they could be sung, along with God Save the King.

In 1937-8 pen portraits of the visitors were introduced, a feature which was resumed after the war.

During hostilities the size and content had perforce to be drastically reduced but the club kept faithful to the supporters and continued to issue programmes despite the difficulties involved. Although comment was limited the programme rarely missed the chance to give an update on the players who had joined the Forces. An advert for Hammonds ales occupied the front cover.

In 1946-7, for one season only, the programme was an elongated shape nine inches top to bottom and three and three-quarter inches across. It was not popular and in succeeding seasons the size returned to the war-time look of eight and-a-half by five and-a-half. In 1947-8 there was blue print on white with a childlike drawing of a goal at the Little Horton End.

Throughout the 1950s when Bradford returned to the Third Division (North) the covers, like the managers, were often being changed. The club colours reverted to green and white and programmes became printed in green on white. Advertisers included Feather Brothers coach trips, Somers furniture and Moffat's fireplaces.

The 1960s saw the arrival of a pocket-size edition, something which attained popularity with many of the lower division clubs. The content was nothing to write at length about but it contained all the basic ingredients for 4d.

From 1966 until the club lost Football League status in 1970, the size increased, but the programme lost much of its individuality as out-of-town printers took on the job of producing the same style of programme for a number of clubs.

As a non-league club the standard dropped and by the end of the 1970-1 season a black and white cover had replaced the colour one. For the final season, 1973-4, the price fell from 3p to 1p and the club ended life with a single sheet issue.

Since the club was re-formed in 1988 much effort has been put into producing a value-for-money issue, and although the price has risen steadily from 50p to £1.50, Tim Clapham, Martin Worthy and most recently Ian Smith have burnt the midnight oil to ensure the Avenue programme has picked up numerous awards.

The early writers of the programme would have been proud of them. It was Tom Maley, Claude Ingram and George Brigg who first devoted time to the work. After the 1939-45 war one of Brigg's assistants in the office, Albert Mortimer, took control and edited the programme for many years. Secretary Brigg continued to oversee matters until he retired in 1973, having occupied his post since 1934.

Special issues down the years include:

England v Ireland (at Park Avenue) - February 1909
Avenue v F.C.Wien (Austria)* - December 1935
Avenue v City (Football League Jubilee) - August 1939
FA v Army (at Park Avenue) - December 1944
Avenue v Partizan (Belgrade), Festival of Britain - May 1951
Avenue v Czechoslovakia (inauguration of floodlights) - October 1961

*First match at Park Avenue against an overseas touring side.

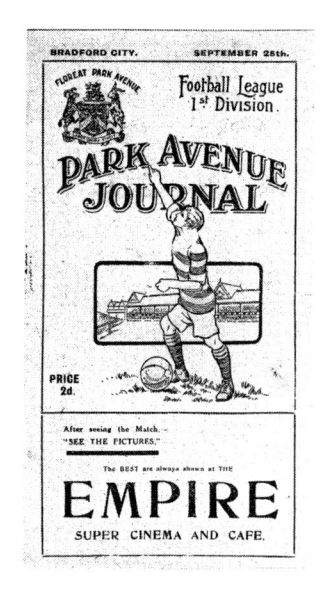

The pointing footballer 24 years apart. Left: a programme for the First division fixture against Bradford City, September 25, 1920. Right: the League North Cup quarter-final against Blackpool and Stanley Matthews, April 8, 1944.

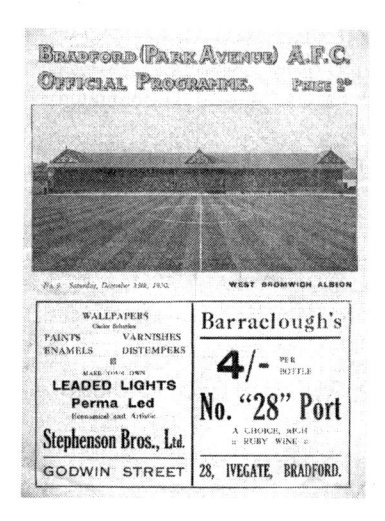

The 1930 programme on the left was more than three times the size (10 x 7 inches) of the pocket programme of 1960-61 (5 x 4 inches)

THEY REPRESENTED BRADFORD

1908-09. Back: G Reid, T Wolstenholme, A Freeborough, D O'Donnell, A Dixon. Next to back: E Hoyle (secretary), G Hubbard (assistant trainer), J Manning, J Donaldson, CT Craig, A Hartwell, R Ward, P Frith (trainer), G Gillies (manager). Seated: P Eccles, C Milnes, T Dilly, T Baddeley, J Dunbavin, T Waterall, R Walton. Front: W Ward, P Milson, H O'Rouke, J Frith, A Fraser, D Donald.

1909-10. Back: F Chadwick (trainer), Gordon, Clark, Handley, Green, Logan, Parker, Mr G Gillies (secretary/manager). Centre: Dyer, Wolstenholme, Crossan, Noble, Smith, Grierson, Manning, Bolton. Front: Donald, Little, McClarence, Dixon, Milnes, Cawdry.

1911-12. Back: R Simpson, unknown, H Dainty, A Watson, A Dixon. Next to back: T Maley (secretary-manager), J Parker, G Buchanan, C Milnes, JH Logan, G Halley, W Kivlichan, F Chadwick (trainer). Seated: D Munro, W Cawdry, T Little, J Turnbull, S Blackham, J Scott, R Mason. Front: D Howie, G Reeves

1913, v Sheffield Wednesday in the FA Cup. Dainty, Buchanan, Munro, Halley, Scott, Watson, Howie, Mr T Maley (manager), Blackham, Mason, Smith, Little, Chadwick (trainer)

1930-31. Back: Allcock, Harkin, Hunter, Robertson, Godfrey, Lloyd. Front: Geldard, Jones, Harwood, Parris, Spooner

1931-32. Back: Cookson, Purdon, Clough, Scott, Robertson, Crayston, Leedham, Parris. Centre: Lister (director), Nuttall (trainer), Ward, Lloyd, Dickinson, Bentley, Dick, Allcock, Rhodes, Godfrey, Morton, Bartlett (assistant trainer), Newby (director), Ingram (secretary/manager). Front: Copley and Berry (directors), Collins (chairman), Smith, Davis, HW Taylor, McMillan, Elwood, GA Taylor, Geldard, Kilcar, Harwood, Greenwood (president), Turner & Brearley (directors)

1932-33: Back: C Godfrey, J Crayston, R Ward, J Bell, T Lloyd, H Nuttall (trainer), J Smith. Front: E Suggett, H Bedford, T Rhodes, S Dickinson, E Parris, J Elwood.

1933-34. Back: Bartlett (assistant trainer), Parris, Ward, McClelland, Crayston, Purdon, Blackmore, Hogan, Hardy (coach). Next to back: Ingram (secretary/manager), Nuttall (trainer), Skaife, Boardman, Kelso, Hawthorn, Bell, Lewis, Godfrey, Berry & Ward (directors). Seated: Newby (director), Turner (chairman), Copley (director), Allcock, Barrett, Lloyd, Danskin, Suggett, Waddilove, Brearley and Ambler (directors). Front: Dickinson, Bowater, Carson, Robertson.

Anyone for golf? At the Northcliffe golf club, Shipley. In the centre is Bill Hardy (manager) and to his left Tommy Lloyd.

1945-46. Back: Greenwood, Stabb, Hepworth, Farr, Taylor, Leonard, Downie, Hallard. Front: Dix, Shackleton, Knott, Danskin, Gibbons, Walker

1946-47. Back: Ure (trainer), McTaff, Stephen, Farr, Farrell, Davidson, Stabb. Front: Smith, Downie, Horsman, Danskin, Gibbons, Donaldson

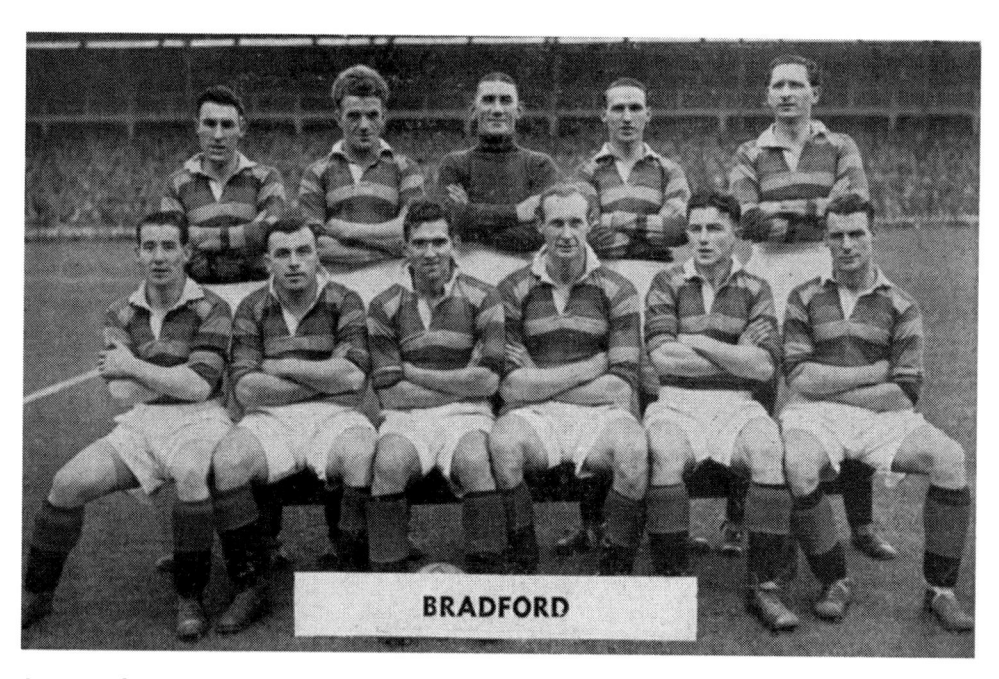

1948-49. Back: Stephen, Horsman, Farr, Farrell, Layton. Front: Glover, Henry, White, Ainsley, Downie, Elliott

1951-52. Back: Suddards, Heffron, Lynn, Hindle, Deplidge, Hudson. Front: Smith, Turner, Crosbie, Wright, Haines.

1953-54. Back: Carlin, Milburn, Whitaker, Begg, Lee, Stainton. Front: Beattie, Brickley, Dunlop, Roberts, Hall

1959-60. Back: Baker, Brims, Hough, Williams, Dick, McCalman. Front: McHard, Harvey, Allan, McAllister, Byrom.

1963-64: Scoular (player-manager), Cook, Dine, McCalman, Flynn, Jones. Front: Burns, Hector, Evans, Atkinson, Bird

1965-66. Back: G Gould, G Turner, J Lumb, G Thomas, E Burns. Middle: J Buchanan (manager), A Bartlett (scout), G Isaacs, J Hardie, P Flynn, P I'anson, G Lightowler, H Gordon, W Rodger, A Symonds, L Padgett (assistant secretary), GH Brigg (secretary). Seated: S Thorp, J Fryatt, K Hector, D McCalman, S Lawrie, R Bird, J Gilpin, C Kaye (trainer)

1968-69. Spiby, Taylor, Hudson, Drury, Hibbitt, Andrews, Down, Lawson, Hardie, Booker, McTigue, Darfield, Walker, Draper, Tanner, Clancy, Robinson

1969-70. Back: Walker, Thom, Saville, Charnley, Hickman, Hardie, Hudson, Dolan, Preece. Front: Henderson, Brannan, Hopkins, Atkinson, Brodie, Beanland, Conley

1972-73. Back: F Beaumont, J Riordan, A Cartwright, P Liney, M Fleming, B Wright, A Leighton (player-manager). Front: J Kay, P Brannan, M Walker, A Smith, W Legg

May 1974, the final team of the old club. Back: Cartwright, Burke, Fleming, Rose, Myers, Peel, Wright. Front: Kay, Walker, the mascot, Jones, Brannan, Bishop.

1988-89. Back: Wright, Hall, Sutcliffe, Hill, Benn, Land, Margison. Front: Waters, McGregor, Hall (player/manager), Tavernier, Armitage, Wigglesworth

1991-92: Eli, Craven, Booth, Watmuff, Stanley, Payton, Wroot, Pickles. Front: Wardman, Edmondson, Gilderdale, Taylor, Pattison

2002-03. Back: Wilson, Hayward, Daly, Mitchell, Turner, Maxwell, Painter, Stansfield. Front: Martin, Atkinson, Quinn, Benn, Prendergast, Lindley, Tracey

2003-04. Back: Wilson, Collins, Hayward, Tracey, Boswell, Maxwell, Crossley, Stansfield, Wood, Wright. Front: James, Quinn, mascot, Benn, mascot, Walsh, Smith, Oleksewycz, Serrant

2004-05. Back: D Helliwell (kit man), Thompson, Jones, Clayton, Colley, Britton, Naylor, Oldham, P Helliwell, Pearce, Roscow (assistant manager). Front: Quinn, Crossley, Oleksewycz, Sherriffe, Shutt (manager), Walsh, Smith, Jones

2005-06. Back: G Brook (manager), W Nazha, T Agus, T Greaves, C Parry, R Siddall, W Benn, D Calcutt, S Newton (reserve team manager), B Crowther (assistant manager). Front: N Heinemann, A Quinn, S Oleksewycz, Doherty, P Mumbly, P Naylor, B Newton, L Brompton, D Walsh, N O'Brien.

2006-07. Back: Illingworth, Shuttleworth, Hoyle, Jeffrey, Allen, Shaw, Ross, Kamara, Mumbly. Front: Smith, Greaves, Connor, Sharpe (manager), Freeman (assistant manager), Chattoe, Redfearn, Tuck, Flynn, Wilson (kit man)

BRADFORD PARK AVENUE IN THE FOOTBALL LEAGUE

	Div	Pos	p	w	d	l	f	a	pts	*home:* w	d	l	f	a	*away:* w	d	l	f	a	
1910	2	*10*	38	17	4	17	64	59	38	12	1	6	47	28	5	3	11	17	31	
1911	2	*12*	38	14	9	15	53	55	37	12	4	3	44	18	2	5	12	9	37	
1912	2	*11*	38	13	9	16	44	45	35	10	5	4	30	16	3	4	12	14	29	
1913	2	*13*	38	14	8	16	60	60	36	12	4	3	47	18	2	4	13	13	42	
1914	2	*2*	38	23	3	12	71	47	49	15	1	3	44	20	8	2	9	27	27	*Promoted*
1915	1	*9*	38	17	7	14	69	65	41	11	4	4	40	20	6	3	10	29	45	
1920	1	*11*	42	15	12	15	60	63	42	8	6	7	31	26	7	6	8	29	37	
1921	1	*22*	42	8	8	26	43	76	24	6	5	10	29	35	2	3	16	14	41	*Relegated*
1922	2	*21*	42	12	9	21	46	62	33	10	5	6	32	22	2	4	15	14	40	*Relegated*
1923	3N	*2*	38	19	9	10	67	38	47	14	4	1	51	15	5	5	9	16	23	
1924	3N	*5*	42	21	10	11	69	43	52	17	3	1	50	12	4	7	10	19	31	
1925	3N	*5*	42	19	12	11	84	42	50	15	5	1	59	13	4	7	10	25	29	
1926	3N	*2*	42	26	8	8	101	43	60	18	2	1	65	10	8	6	7	36	33	
1927	3N	*3*	42	24	7	11	101	59	55	18	3	0	74	21	6	4	11	27	38	
1928	3N	*1*	42	27	9	6	101	45	63	18	2	1	68	22	9	7	5	33	23	*Promoted*
1929	2	*3*	42	22	4	16	88	70	48	18	2	1	62	22	4	2	15	26	48	
1930	2	*4*	42	19	12	11	91	70	50	14	5	2	65	28	5	7	9	26	42	
1931	2	*6*	42	18	10	14	97	66	46	15	4	2	71	24	3	6	12	26	42	
1932	2	*6*	42	21	7	14	72	63	49	17	2	2	44	18	4	5	12	28	45	
1933	2	*8*	42	17	8	17	77	71	42	13	4	4	51	27	4	4	13	26	44	
1934	2	*5*	42	23	3	16	86	67	49	16	2	3	63	27	7	1	13	23	40	
1935	2	*15*	42	11	16	15	55	63	38	7	8	6	32	28	4	8	9	23	35	
1936	2	*16*	42	14	9	19	62	84	37	13	6	2	43	26	1	3	17	19	58	
1937	2	*20*	42	12	9	21	52	88	33	10	4	7	33	33	2	5	14	19	55	
1938	2	*7*	42	17	9	16	69	56	43	13	4	4	51	22	4	5	12	18	34	
1939	2	*17*	42	12	11	19	61	82	35	8	6	7	33	35	4	5	12	28	47	
1947	2	*16*	42	14	11	17	65	77	39	7	6	8	29	28	7	5	9	36	49	
1948	2	*14*	42	16	8	18	68	72	40	11	3	7	45	30	5	5	11	23	42	
1949	2	*17*	42	13	11	18	65	78	37	8	8	5	37	26	5	3	13	28	52	
1950	2	*22*	42	10	11	21	51	77	31	7	6	8	34	34	3	5	13	17	43	*Relegated*
1951	3N	*6*	46	23	8	15	90	72	54	15	3	5	46	23	8	5	10	44	49	
1952	3N	*8*	46	19	12	15	74	64	50	13	6	4	51	28	6	6	11	23	36	
1953	3N	*7*	46	19	12	15	75	61	50	10	8	5	37	23	9	4	10	38	38	
1954	3N	*9*	46	18	14	14	77	68	50	13	6	4	57	31	5	8	10	20	37	
1955	3N	*16*	46	15	11	20	56	70	41	11	7	5	29	21	4	4	15	27	49	
1956	3N	*23*	46	13	7	26	61	122	33	13	4	6	47	38	0	3	20	14	84	
1957	3N	*20*	46	16	3	27	66	93	35	11	2	10	41	40	5	1	17	25	53	
1958	3N	*22*	46	13	11	22	68	95	37	8	6	9	41	41	5	5	13	27	54	
1959	4	*14*	46	18	7	21	75	77	43	15	1	7	51	29	3	6	14	24	48	
1960	4	*11*	46	17	15	14	70	68	49	12	10	1	48	25	5	5	13	22	43	
1961	4	*4*	46	26	8	12	84	74	60	16	5	2	49	22	10	3	10	35	52	*Promoted*
1962	3	*11*	46	20	7	19	80	78	47	13	5	5	47	27	7	2	14	33	51	
1963	3	*21*	46	14	12	20	79	97	40	10	9	4	43	36	4	3	16	36	61	*Relegated*
1964	4	*13*	46	18	9	19	75	81	45	13	5	5	50	34	5	4	14	25	47	
1965	4	*7*	46	20	17	9	86	62	57	14	8	1	52	22	6	9	8	34	40	
1966	4	*11*	46	21	5	20	102	92	47	14	2	7	59	31	7	3	13	43	61	
1967	4	*23*	46	11	13	22	52	79	35	7	6	10	30	34	4	7	12	22	45	
1968	4	*24*	46	4	15	27	30	82	23	3	7	13	18	35	1	8	14	12	47	
1969	4	*24*	46	5	10	31	32	106	20	5	8	10	19	34	0	2	21	13	72	
1970	4	*24*	46	6	11	29	41	96	23	6	5	12	23	32	0	6	17	18	64	

PLAYERS WITH 200 FOOTBALL LEAGUE GAMES

		D.o.b	Birthplace	First Seas	Apps	Subs	Gls	From	To
Atkinson C	Charlie	17/12/1932	Hull	1956	339	0	50	Hull City	Bradford City
Taylor HW	Harold	18/11/1902	Frizinghall	1921	334	0	15	Amateur	Southport
Lloyd T	Tommy	17/11/1903	Wednesbury	1927	328	0	17	Sunderland	Burton Town
Suddards J	Jeff	17/01/1929	Bradford	1949	327	0	0	Hull City	Cambridge City
Howie D	David	15/07/1886	Galston	1911	306	0	21	Kilmarnock	retired
Farr TF	Chick	19/02/1914	Bathgate	1934	297	0	0	Blackburn Ath.	retired
McCalman DS	Don	18/10/1935	Greenock	1959	297	0	5	Hibernian	Barrow
Deplidge W	Bill	12/11/1924	Bradford	1946	274	0	62	App.	Yeovil Town
Scattergood EO	Ernie	29/05/1887	Riddings	1914	268	0	5	Derby County	Alfreton Town
Hardie JC	John	07/02/1938	Edinburgh	1963	265	0	0	Chester	Crystal Palace
Danskin R	Bob	28/05/1908	Scotswood	1932	263	0	4	Leeds United	retired
McLean G	George	24/08/1897	Forfar	1921	250	0	135	Forfar	Huddersfield T
Scott JMA	Jack		Motherwell	1909	244	0	3	Hamilton Ac.	Manchester Utd.
Horsman L	Les	26/05/1920	Burley-in-Wharfedale	1946	239	0	18	Guiseley	Halifax Town
Little TSC	Tommy	27/02/1890	Ilford	1908	231	0	108	Southend Utd.	Stoke City
Blackham S	Sam	19/08/1890	Edmonton	1911	221	0	0	Barrow	Halifax Town
Clough JH	Jack	13/05/1902	Murton	1926	208	0	0	Middlesbrough	Mansfield Town
Turnbull RJ	Bobby	17/12/1895	South Bank	1919	208	0	47	South Bank	Leeds United
Lightowler GB	Gerry	05/09/1940	Bradford	1958	207	2	1	Amateur	Bradford City
Peel HB	Harold	26/03/1900	Bradford	1920	207	0	38	Calverley	Arsenal
Hindle FJ	Frank	22/06/1925	Blackburn	1950	204	0	0	Chester	Barrow
Smith JW	Jackie	27/05/1920	St Pancras	1945	204	0	26	Avro Works	Grantham

PLAYERS WITH 50 FOOTBALL LEAGUE GOALS

		D.o.b	Birthplace	First Seas	Apps	Subs	Gls	From	To
McLean G	George	24/08/1897	Forfar	1921	250	0	136	Forfar	Huddersfield T
McDonald K	Ken	24/04/1898	Llanrwst	1923	145	0	135	Manchester Utd.	Hull City
Hector KJ	Kevin	02/11/1944	Leeds	1962	176	0	113	Juniors	Derby County
Little TSC	Tommy	27/02/1890	Ilford	1908	231	0	108	Southend Utd.	Stoke City
Crosbie RC	Bob	02/09/1925	Glasgow	1949	139	0	72	Bury	Hull City
Buchanan J	Jock	09/06/1928	Underwood, Stirling	1957	164	0	67	Derby County	retired
Bauchop JR	Jimmy	22/05/1886	Sauchie	1913	157	0	67	Tottenham H	Lincoln City
Lewis TH	Tommy	11/10/1909	Ellesmere Port	1933	193	0	66	Wrexham	Blackpool
Deplidge W	Bill	12/11/1924	Bradford	1946	274	0	62	App.	Yeovil Town
Robertson JH	Jimmy	22/03/1913	Berwick-on-Tweed	1932	130	0	59	Welbeck Coll.	Bradford City
Quantrill AE	Alf	22/01/1897	Punjab, India	1924	191	0	58	Preston NE	Nottm. Forest
Ham RS	Bobby	29/03/1942	Bradford	1959	159	0	53	Juniors	Huddersfield T
Allan J	John	23/03/1931	Stirling	1958	70	0	51	Third Lanark	Halifax Town
Atkinson C	Charlie	17/12/1932	Hull	1956	339	0	50	Hull City	Bradford City